ON BEING A TEACHER

third edition

jeffrey a. kottler
stanley j. zehm
ellen kottler

ON BEING A TEACHER

the human dimension

third edition

CORWIN PRESS
A SAGE Publications Company
Thousand Oaks, California

For information:

Corwin Press
A Sage Publications Company
2455 Teller Road
Thousand Oaks, California 91320
www.corwinpress.com

Sage Publications Ltd
1 Oliver's Yard
55 City Road
London EC1Y 1SP
United Kingdom

Sage Publications India Pvt. Ltd.
B-42, Panchsheel Enclave
Post Box 4109
New Delhi 110 017 India

Printed in the United States of America

Library of Congress Cataloging-in-Publication Data

Kottler, Jeffrey A.
On being a teacher : the human dimension / Jeffrey A. Kottler, Stanley J. Zehm, Ellen Kottler.— 3rd ed.
    p. cm.
Includes bibliographical references and index.
ISBN 0-7619-3943-1 (cloth) — ISBN 0-7619-3944-X (pbk.)
    1. Teaching. 2. Motivation in education.
3. Teachers. I. Zehm, Stanley J. II. Kottler, Ellen. III. Title.
LB1025.3.Z44 2005
371.1—dc22

                                        2004022983

This book is printed on acid-free paper.

05   06   07   08   10   9   8   7   6   5   4   3   2   1

Acquisitions editor:	Rachel Livsey
Editorial assistant:	Phyllis Cappello
Production editor:	Sanford Robinson
Copy editor:	Terese Platten
Typesetter:	C&M Digitals (P) Ltd.
Cover designer:	Anthony Paular
Indexer:	Sheila Bodell

Contents

Preface to
the Third Edition

The third edition of *On Being a Teacher* has been prepared to provide preservice, beginning, and veteran teachers with resources they will need to provide caring and competent instruction, as well as guidance, to students of all ages. As teachers interact with their students and colleagues, establishing and improving their relationships are critical to achieving and maintaining success in the classroom. Students want teachers who care about them and demonstrate their care. With the ever present need to attract new teachers and keep veteran teachers in the profession, we hope to support and nurture positive interactions. Building and sustaining relationships are the basis for the rewards of the teaching profession.

One of the most discouraging trends of present times is that about one third of all teachers are leaving the profession within three years. The need for minority teachers is even more critical considering the increasing diversity of our classrooms. We also find many veteran teachers are finding their enthusiasm for serving young people eroded and are leaving the teaching ranks. Most of these unhappy teachers began their career filled with optimism and enthusiasm for teaching. They were just like you—excited, eager, and passionately committed to making a difference in others' lives. They were certainly not lured by promises of high wages or annual bonuses. So, what happened to tarnish the professional aspirations of these beginning and veteran teachers? What caused them to walk away from their commitments to our nation's youth?

The third edition of this book explores the human resources you need as a teacher, not only to survive in this work, but to flourish. Our aim is to help you renew each day your commitment to reach and teach each of the students committed to your caring and competent instruction.

An Overview

There are many books written in the field of education that speak to practicing teachers and prospective educators about the methods and materials of instruction. Such texts and manuals address every facet of instructional methods, environmental control, motivational strategies, behavior management, discipline, curriculum development, assessment, and technological resources that are available. Yet, the single most important human resource is a teacher's own personal qualities—his or her unique style of interaction and personality.

All great teachers have been influential and inspirational to others not because of their training in materials and methods, but rather because of the internal human resources they were able to call on to give life to their meaningful messages. The best teachers are those who are able to translate their knowledge, wisdom, and experience into a form of communication that is compelling and interesting. Although teachers know that content is important, students couldn't care less what teachers are teaching; what matters most to students is the style in which such knowledge and wisdom are imparted.

On Being a Teacher is designed to address the neglected but crucial aspect of what makes educators most effective. It is a book that speaks directly to students and practitioners of education who wish to become clearer about what being a superlative teacher is all about—not the mechanics of instruction, but the essence of what has made all great teachers so powerful in commanding attention, respect, and devotion from their students. It is about those unique human resources that others find so inspirational, that motivate people to go beyond their perceived limits and help them to find answers to the questions that are most significant.

The following themes contained in this book are designed to inspire newcomers to the profession in a number of ways: (a) Good teachers take care of themselves, as well as their students; (b) given the appropriate classroom environment, students can learn to take care of one another; (c) greater awareness of cultural and individual differences helps teachers to be more responsive to the needs of an increasingly diverse population; (d) teachers are often called upon to do so much more than impart knowledge—they influence children through the quality of their relationships and the power of their personalities; (e) a reflective perspective can help teachers to create the image of the kind of teacher *they* want to be, creating an impetus to help them reach their goals; and (f) all educational practitioners, no matter how uncertain they are about their potential, can learn to become more effective as communicators and more responsive as professional helpers.

THE AUDIENCE

This book could be used as a text in a variety of teacher education classes, beginning as well as advanced. The previous edition has been adopted by instructors in courses ranging from introduction to elementary or secondary education to a variety of teaching methods classes and teaching practica; it has also been used as a resource for those in early childhood and higher education.

Another arena in which this book has proven useful is in the context of teacher induction programs for beginning teachers. It is addressed as well to administrators who wish to inspire their staff members to become more invigorated in their daily work. It also speaks directly to practicing teachers who have longed to find ways to access more of their own humanity, compassion, and creativity. Most of all, it is directed to those professional educators and those who aspire to such a calling who wish to mobilize their greatest gifts—their caring and compassion—in service to others.

THE CONTENTS

In Chapter 1, we describe the essence of what makes a teacher truly great—those human qualities and characteristics that inspire others to go beyond their limited expectations. It is our contention that to achieve excellence in this profession, it is also necessary for teachers to be personally effective in their own lives. If you believe that it is important for your students to be inquisitive, creative, hardworking, constructive risk takers, and compassionate and moral citizens, the question to ask yourself is how you are living those same qualities in your own life.

Being a fully functioning human will be the primary resource you will call upon daily to demonstrate to students those concepts and skills most crucial to their learning. In Chapter 2, we discuss how this modeling process takes place in the human dimensions of learning. Our job is to teach people, not content areas. To do this well, we must help children to integrate what they are learning into their own lives—to make material meaningful and personally relevant.

Chapters 3 and 4 are about verbal and nonverbal communication, the core of all effective teaching. We invite present and future teachers to explore their own strengths and weaknesses in relating to others. These chapters aim at assisting teachers, regardless of their present levels of confidence and proficiency, to construct a plan to improve their effectiveness as communicators and experts in developing helpful relationships.

Whereas the previous chapters focus on the more general subject of reaching others through verbal interaction, Chapter 5 concentrates specifically on the skills of helping. We review for teachers those behaviors that are most likely to help them to reach students on multiple levels. We cover the basics of dealing with student problems and emotional pain as well as handling conflict and confrontation. We urge teachers to become experts not only in the methods of pedagogy and in the content areas of the curriculum but also in the art and science of guiding human beings, their moral and emotional maturity as well as their intellectual and physical development.

Chapter 6 focuses on what teachers struggle with the most: the obstacles that make this career so challenging. These include such things as the limitations of the school environment; sabotaging elements in the child's home environment; the stresses of interpersonal relationships with administrators, colleagues, and difficult children; and esteem issues, as well as the lack of teacher efficacy.

Chapter 7 is about the predictable stresses and strains that teachers often experience in their careers. Rather than "burning out" as a flame might die, many teachers slowly, inexorably "rust out." We deal with the subject of staying vibrant and impassioned about teaching in order to avoid turning into an embittered and frustrated veteran who counts the years until retirement. This preparation begins now, early in one's professional career, not after oxidation has already worn away morale.

Chapter 7 also offers advice to beginners and experienced teachers alike on ways to remain passionately committed to their calling. We suggest ways for teachers to keep learning and growing, to take constructive risks, and to take care of themselves so that they will flourish in this wonderful field of education. In Chapter 8, we continue this theme by challenging practicing and prospective teachers to become more reflective as they grow as persons and professionals. What we know about the best teachers is that *they* make it a priority in their lives to ask themselves continuously what they are doing and why, and what builds meaning for them and for others.

Finally, in the last chapter, we ask teachers to create an image of the persons and professionals they want to be one year from now and 5, 15, and 30 years from now. It is only through constructing such goals for yourself, and working hard to reach them, that you will ever become the truly great educator you would like to be, the kind of teacher children will remember throughout their lives.

This edition features the addition of Ellen Kottler as a third author since Stan Zehm died before the previous edition could be completed. Ellen's contribution in updating the book has been to include a variety of specific teaching strategies for practitioners to consider in their classrooms, as well as suggested professional development activities at the end of each chapter.

There have been a number of additions throughout the book. New to Chapter 1 is the introduction of No Child Left Behind legislation and its impact. Chapter 2 has been lengthened to include a description of the diversity found in today's classrooms with sections on learning styles and multiple intelligences. Chapter 3 now features a discussion of how and when to make a referral to a specialist and an identification of relationship specialists in the school. The Chapter 4 focus on building relationships now includes the process for holding morning meetings for elementary school teachers and structuring democratic classrooms. It also has a segment on communication with parents and guardians with an in-depth look at how to hold a parent/guardian conference. Chapter 6 has been expanded to include a look at the demands on teachers' time. Chapter 7 features a section on research-based strategies for classroom management. New to Chapter 8 are guides for individual reflection and for group reflection. The book ends with an emphasis on commitment. Chapter 9 is updated to review benefits of induction programs and ways for teachers to become involved in their schools and districts and seek professional development through further education as well as professional organizations.

ACKNOWLEDGMENTS

The contributions of the following reviewers are gratefully acknowledged:

Dr. Dottie Bauer
Associate Professor
Education, Special Education,
Early Childhood
Keene State College
Keene, NH

Michelle Barnea, RN, MS Ed
Early Childhood Consultant
Independent Consultant
Millburn, NJ

Pat Carlin
Localization Project Manager
Lexmark, International
Kentucky Department of Education
Lexington, KY

Dr. Rose Weiss
Adjunct Professor
Nova Southeastern University
Fort Lauderdale, FL

and the dedicated professionals at Corwin Press: Rachel Livsey, Phyllis Cappello, and Sanford Robinson.

About the Authors

Jeffrey A. Kottler has worked as a teacher, counselor, and professor in a variety of settings, including hospitals, mental health centers, schools, clinics, universities, corporations, and private practice. He is the author or coauthor of over 55 books in education and psychology, including *Beyond Blame: A New Way of Resolving Conflicts in Relationships* (1994), *The Language of Tears* (1996), *What's Really Said in the Teachers Lounge: Provocative Ideas About Cultures and Classrooms* (1997), *Succeeding With Difficult Students* (1997), *Counseling Tips for Elementary School Principals* (1998), *Counseling Skills for Teachers* (2000), *Nuts and Bolts of Helping* (2000), *Making Changes Last* (2001), *On Being a Therapist* (2003), *American Shaman* (2004), and *Secrets for Secondary School Teachers: How to Succeed in Your First Year* (2004).

Jeffrey is Professor and Chair of the Counseling Department at California State University, Fullerton. He has served as a Fulbright Scholar in Peru and Iceland and lectures widely throughout the world.

Stanley J. Zehm was Professor and former Chair of Instructional and Curricular Studies at the University of Nevada, Las Vegas, prior to his death in 1999. He also worked as Adjunct Professor at Heritage College, where he had previously served as Dean of Education. He worked as both an elementary and secondary teacher for 15 years and as a counselor, and he held several administrative positions, including superintendent.

He earned his doctorate in English education from Stanford University. He also possessed degrees and specialized training in philosophy, counseling, English, and theology. In addition to his experience in schools, he practiced as a family and child counselor.

He was the author of numerous articles in professional journals, as well as several books for teachers and school administrators.

Ellen Kottler was a secondary school teacher for over 25 years in public, private, and alternative school settings teaching a range of courses in social studies, humanities, and Spanish. She also served as an administrative specialist in curriculum and professional development for the Clark County School District (Las Vegas, Nevada). She is the author or coauthor of books for educators including *Counseling Skills for Teachers* (2000), *Children With Limited English: Teaching Strategies for the Regular Classroom* (2002), and *Secrets for Secondary School Teachers: How to Succeed in Your First Year* (2004).

Ellen is a Lecturer in the Department of Secondary Education at California State University, Fullerton, and a grant writer for the Anaheim Union High School District (Anaheim, California).

Postscript and Dedication

S tan Zehm died within two days of finishing the second edition of this book. His heart failed him at a time in his life when he was enjoying his most productive and fulfilling years—as a teacher, writer, father, husband, and grandfather. He was one of my dearest friends and I can't write these words without feeling the terrible loss.

Stan embodied all this book represents. He lived it with his heart and soul. His own heart, while physically frail, was committed totally to his family, his students and colleagues, and his friends. He is missed deeply, but his spirit lives on in the words that follow.

I dedicate this book to the memory of Stanley Zehm, the greatest teacher I have ever known.

J. A. K.

CHAPTER ONE

On Being a Teacher

Who was the best teacher you ever had? Which mentor immediately stands out as the one who has been most influential and inspirational in your life? This could have been a teacher from elementary school, or high school, or college. It could be a coach or a neighbor or a relative. Whoever it was, your teacher was someone who was an absolute master at helping you learn far more than you ever imagined possible.

B ring to mind a clear image of this remarkable teacher. Hear your teacher's voice, concentrating on not only its unique resonance and tone but also some special message that still haunts you. Feel the inspiration that still lives within you as a result of your relationship with this teacher. Think about the personal qualities this person exuded that commanded your respect and reverence.

As you recall memories of this individual who was such a powerful model in your life, it is likely that you can identify and list certain personal characteristics that were most powerful. As you review this list of qualities, it may surprise you to realize that very few of these notable attributes have to do with the content of what this teacher taught or even with personal teaching methods.

What is ironic about this phenomenon is that much of teacher preparation continues to be focused on methods courses and in areas of content specialty. The assumption behind this training for elementary and secondary teachers is that when you study a subject in depth and learn the proper methods of instruction, presumably you then become a more competent and outstanding teacher. Not included in this process are a number of other variables that make up the essence of all great educators and infuse them with power—their distinctly human dimensions, including personality traits, attitudes, and relationship skills.

This is not to say that the best educators are not experts in their fields, because they are. Current legislation under the No Child Left Behind Act of 2001 calls for a "highly qualified" teacher in every classroom by the end of the 2005–2006 school year and the use of research-based practices (Ryan & Cooper, 2004; Yell & Drasgow, 2005.) Teachers in core academic areas must be licensed by their state demonstrating they possess content knowledge through college coursework, examination, or through a process in which the district examines teacher qualifications in terms of subject expertise known as the "high objective uniform state standard of evaluation" or HOUSSE. The core academic areas are English, reading-language arts, mathematics, science, foreign languages, civics, government, economics, art, history, and geography. There are some outstanding resources to help build your technical expertise (see Bellon, Bellon, & Blank, 1992; Borich, 2004; Johnson & Johnson, 1999; Joyce, Weil, Calhoun, & Joyce, 2003; Slavin, 2002), as well as solid advice from master practitioners (see Gill, 1998; Kottler, Kottler, & Kottler, 2004; Palmer, 1998; Scheidecker & Freeman, 1999; Stone, 1999). Nor are we implying that it is possible to be a superlative teacher, coach, mentor, or parent without extensive knowledge of human learning and mastery of interpersonal communication. But all the knowledge and skills in the world are virtually useless to teachers who cannot convey their meaning to learners in a personally designed way. Likewise, all the methods crammed into a teacher's bag of tricks are of little help to someone who cannot translate their value in a style that commands others' attention and influences their behavior.

It is the human dimension that gives all teachers, whether in the classroom, the sports arena, or the home, their power as effective influencers. When you review the list of qualities that made your best teachers effective, you probably noticed that so much of what made a difference in your life was not what they did, but who they were as human beings. They exhibited certain characteristics that helped you to trust them, to believe in them. It did not matter whether they taught physics or ballet, grammar or bicycle repair; you would sit at their feet and listen, enraptured by the magic they could create with the spoken word and with their actions. They could get you to do things that you never dreamed were possible. It was not so much that you cared deeply about what they were teaching as that you found yourself so intrigued by them as people. You respected them and felt connected to them in some profound way that transcended the content of their instruction. You responded to their example and encouragement. You began to see dimensions of yourself you were previously unaware of—special gifts, skills, ideas. Under their caring instruction, you began to know and value your unique self and find confidence in your personal voice.

NEGLECT OF THE HUMAN DIMENSIONS OF TEACHING

In spite of your own personal experiences in being profoundly influenced by mentors and teachers who were eccentric, unique, or otherwise showed a distinctive character, there has not been a lot of attention directed to this important subject. In a classic handbook for teachers, Arthur Jersild (1955) was among the first of modern-day educators to focus attention on the connection between teachers' personal lives and their professional effectiveness. Jersild maintained that understanding yourself is the single most important task in the growth toward developing healthy attitudes of self-acceptance. The basic idea is that to help others, you must be intimately aware of your own strengths and limitations so that you can present yourself in ways that are optimally effective.

The influence of Jersild's little book was short-lived. Soon after it was published, Sputnik, the first space vehicle, was launched by the Soviet Union. The United States began a frenzied focus not on teachers' needs, but on the perceived national security imperative to train teachers of scientists and technicians. The human dimensions of teaching were considered too soft to be of great priority.

In the 1960s, during the brief moments of "The Great Society" and its relevance in education, writers and researchers began to pay more attention to the human aspects of teaching and learning. Carl Rogers (1939, 1969a, 1980), a strong voice for a focus on self in teacher education, wrote extensively about the need for teachers to be process oriented rather than exclusively content oriented in their approach. This means spending time in the class discussing not only the poems of Emily Dickinson, the location of national capitals, or the nervous system, but also how children feel about these subjects, about themselves in relation to their learning, and about one another as they continue the dialogue. According to Rogers, teachers must spend considerable time and effort building positive relationships with children, allowing their authenticity, genuineness, and caring to shine through. When these human dimensions are cultivated, a teacher can genuinely act as a "person, not a faceless embodiment of a curricular requirement, or a sterile pipe through which knowledge is passed from one generation to the next" (Rogers, 1969b, p. 107).

As the 1960s came to an end, there began a gradual and continuing shift toward the technology of teaching, as championed by B. F. Skinner and the behaviorists. In opposition to the view of Rogers, Skinner asserted that teachers fail not because of any human limitations, but because they are not prepared to manage student behaviors (Skinner, 1969, p. 167). Many useful research efforts soon followed to develop a technology of classroom behavior management, although a side effect of this effort was that the more human aspects of education were criticized as imprecise and unnecessary.

One singular exception to this neglect of the human dimensions of education in the 1970s was presented by Angelo Boy and Gerald Pine (1971) in their book on the personal growth of teachers. They were convinced that continuous, balanced development in human, vocational, spiritual, and recreational areas was essential for all teachers to thrive in their work and lives. They also made the compelling point that the goal of education is not to teach subject matter but to promote the development of productive and positive human beings. They contended that the teacher must be well adjusted and well prepared professionally in order to nurture these qualities in others.

With the advent of the 1980s, the accountability measures of Reaganomics, and the plethora of "nation-at-risk" types of reports, attention was further drawn away from a focus on growing teachers as human beings as well as professionals. Several other phenomena during the 1980s also contributed to the failure to focus on the human aspects of our profession. The first was a conservative religious response to anything in education that could even be remotely associated with *secular humanism*, a philosophy that emphasized freedom and permissiveness. Many teacher educators who believed in building a solid professional base on a strong, mature human foundation were fearful of being branded secular humanists.

The "Yuppie" phenomenon was a second factor that prevented others from focusing on the human dimension of teaching, due to the selfish, materialistic fascination of the "me generation." Finally, the popularity of the so-called effective schools movement riveted the attention of North American educators on classroom climate, academic expectations, administrative leadership, and high test scores. There was little room in the effective schools model for consideration of human dimensions of teaching and learning, which were thought to be tangential.

The 1980s were years of great promise, but with little personal or professional payoff for teachers. During this nerve-wracking decade for education, there were many books and articles written about reducing stress and avoiding burnout (as examples, see Humphrey & Humphrey, 1986; Swick, 1985). There were, however, few systematic attempts to aid understanding and strategies for cultivating the human dimension of teachers.

The 1990s provided a more fertile field for attending to the human aspects of what it means to be a teacher. There were several signals indicative of a grassroots readiness and demand for attention to the human side of the educational endeavor. The call for restructuring and reform in education was based on the shared convictions of teachers and administrators that unless educators were empowered to shape the personal and professional dimensions of the educational enterprise, there would be no durable reform of education.

This decade also placed an emphasis on multicultural education (see Campbell & Delgado-Campbell, 2000; Hernandez, 2000; Manning & Baruth, 1999; Noel, 1999) and constructivist teaching (see Henderson, 1996; Mintzes, Wandersee, & Novak, 1998; Selley, 1999). These unusually "human" dimensions of learning represented a significant expansion of humanistic philosophy in that rather than stressing individual perceptions, they adopted a "postmodern" view of learning as influenced and shaped by one's culture and language.

Many of the hoped-for reforms of the 1990s, including site-based management of schools, empowerment of teachers, charter schools, revitalization of inner-city schools, bilingual learning for all students, national performance standards, accelerated learning programs, and a number of other national and local initiatives to improve education, produced limited degrees of success. The 1990s were so mired in divisive partisan political battles that the needs of teachers went largely ignored.

Currently, under the No Child Left Behind (NCLB) Act of 2001, the focus of education is on stronger school accountability as measured by annual testing of student achievement (Goldberg, 2004). States are required to administer standards-based reading and mathematics assessments in grades 3 through 8 and at one grade level 10 through 12 during the 2005–2006 school year, adding science assessments during 2007–2008 at least once at the elementary, middle, and high school level. Additionally, schools must raise student achievement levels to meet annual objectives so that students will meet set levels of proficiency or face a series of consequences and disaggregate the data by student subgroups to track achievement for all students in order to close achievement gaps. Progress is reported in annual school report cards, and results serve as the basis for determining promotion, graduation, financing, and school governance. As a consequence of these high stakes tests, teachers today are learning to use data-driven analysis of test scores to design their lessons to make sure students meet or exceed the standards on which their students will be tested. Perhaps lost in the focus on accountability are the human dimensions of teaching.

There is no doubt that this is a complicated law. Yell and Drasgow (2005) note that although NCLB increases the amount of federal funding by 25%, it increases the role of the federal government in education with its mandates for states, school districts, schools, and teachers. The main implications of these measures for teachers are in the need for expertise in raising student achievement in "(a) developing and using progress monitoring and data collection systems, and (b) matching instruction programs and strategies to students' progress" (Yell & Drasgow, 2005, p. 117).

The pressures teachers face under "test-based accountability policies" are resulting in a narrowing of information and educational experience for students (Goldberg, 2004; Pedulla, 2003). It is no surprise that "Teachers are spending a sizable amount of instructional time to prepare students for state tests." (Abrams & Madaus, 2003, p. 35). They develop and administer pre-tests and post-tests for units of study and quarterly benchmark tests to track the progress or lack of progress of their students and deliver remediation as needed. It is not uncommon for schools to offer a second period in a given subject, for example, math, to provide students with additional support.

With respect to student relationships, in the March 2003 issue of *Educational Leadership*, published by the Association for

Supervision and Curriculum Development, which notably devoted the issue to creating caring schools, Schaps (2003) states "Community building should become—at a minimum—a strong complement to the prevailing focus on academic achievement." Schaps notes that " . . . the evidence for the importance of building caring school communities is clear and compelling" (Schaps 2003, p. 33). Additionally, Bryk and Schneider (2003) review the literature that supports building relational trust as the link bringing individuals together as a source of school reform. "Distinct role relationships characterize the social exchanges of schooling: teachers with students, teachers with other teachers, teachers with parents, and all groups with the school principal" (Bryk and Scheider, 2003, p. 41). Schools with daily productive exchanges in a safe and secure environment that recognize respect, personal regard, individual responsibility, and personal integrity are more likely to have improvements in student achievement.

In spite of the limited successes in the past and the challenges of high-stakes testing today, we remain optimistic that we are entering a more enlightened age that more genuinely attends to the preparation of the whole teacher. It seems clear, not only from our own experience, but from others' as well, that being a teacher involves a special blend of personal dimensions combined with technical and instructional expertise. What you do is certainly important, but so is who you are.

ATTRIBUTES OF A GREAT TEACHER

There may be considerable debate among educational theoreticians and practitioners about the optimal curriculum, the most appropriate philosophy of teaching for today's schools, the best methods of instruction and strategies for discipline, but there is a reasonable consensus about what makes a teacher great, even if these characteristics are uniquely expressed.

Take a minute away from your reading and reflect on how you ended up where you are right now. What inspired you, or rather *who* inspired you, to consider teaching as a profession? It is likely that you had both negative and positive models—those who struck you as absolutely hopeless as teachers, as well as those who were true masters. If you are like most of us, you are taking this course of study right now because one or more of your own teachers had certain attributes that you greatly admired. In fact, you so envied their lives and work that you are now following in their footsteps.

On your personal list—on almost anyone's agenda—is a collection of those human characteristics that are common to the best teachers. These are the attributes that regardless of subject area, instructional methods, and educational assignment, supply the energy behind the ability to influence others in constructive ways. The extent to which you can work to develop these same human dimensions in yourself will determine how effective you will be as a mentor to others and how satisfied you will feel with your choice to be, or to continue to be, part of this profession.

As we review the personal and professional dimensions of what makes teachers great, we are not so much encouraging you to compare yourself to this ideal as we are suggesting that you take inventory of your personal functioning to assess your own strengths and weaknesses. Such an honest self-examination can help you to identify unexpressed potential that is lying dormant in you—reserves of positive energy just waiting for you to activate them.

Take comfort in the reality that there are really many ways that a teacher can capitalize on personal dimensions to help and inspire others. You have witnessed extraordinary instructors who were loud and dramatic and others who were soft and understated. You have had great teachers who were kind and supportive and others who were stern and demanding. You have enjoyed the benefits of working with teachers who were great speakers; others who were captivating one-on-one; and still others who excelled in small, informal groups. You have known wonderful teachers who may, at first, seem to be quite different in their style and personality, yet what they all had in common is that they found ways to maximize their personal strengths. With considerable reflection and some preparation, you can do the same thing.

The decision to be, or to continue to be, a teacher is one with far-reaching consequences. You have committed yourself not only to a lifestyle in which you must become an expert in your field, but also to one in which you have tremendous incentives to be the most well adjusted, fully functioning, and satisfied human being you can possibly be. What exactly does that involve? Return to your own experiences with the best teachers you ever had. Think again about their personal characteristics that you believe made the most difference to you. Compare these attributes with those in the following paragraphs. This is not intended to be an exhaustive list, but rather a sampling of what many people mention as most significant. As you review these qualities, consider the extent to which you are working to develop them more in yourself.

Charisma

Since the beginning of human time, those who were tapped for the calling of teacher, whether as priests, professors, or poets, were those who had developed the capacity to inspire others. They emanated a personality force that others found attractive, compelling, even seductive in the sense that there was a strong desire to know more about and from them. In the words of the novelist and former teacher Pat Conroy (1982), charisma in teachers occurs when they allow their personality to shine through their subject matter:

> I developed the Great Teacher Theory late in my freshman year. It was a cornerstone of the theory that great teachers had great personalities and that the greatest teachers had outrageous personalities. I did not like decorum or rectitude in a classroom; I preferred a highly oxygenated atmosphere, a climate of intemperance, rhetoric, and feverish melodrama. And I wanted my teachers to make me smart. A great teacher is my adversary, my conqueror, commissioned to chastise me. He leaves me tame and grateful for the new language he has purloined from other Kings whose granaries are famous. He tells me that teaching is the art of theft: of knowing what to steal and from whom. (p. 271)

Scholars may argue as to whether qualities such as charisma are ingrained or can be learned. We would prefer to sidestep that debate and suggest that all those who have devoted their lives to the service of others can increase charismatic powers and thereby command attention in the classroom. This is true whether your inclination is to be dramatic or low key in your presentations, loud or soft. Charisma, after all, can be displayed in so many different ways, depending on your personal style, not to mention what your students respond to best. It involves gaining access to your own unique assets as a human being, which allows you to find a voice that is authentic, compelling, and captivating.

Randi, for example, is not the kind of person one would ordinarily describe as "magnetic." She is typically quiet and soft-spoken, usually content to hang out on the perimeter of most discussions that take place at parties or in the teachers' lounge. That is not to say that she is not thoughtful and articulate; it is just that she prefers to express herself with restraint, at least when she is around other adults. What most of Randi's friends and family would be surprised to discover is how different she can be behind the closed door of her classroom.

Randi realized long ago that although it is her natural inclination to be somewhat muted, even passive, in her daily interactions, there is no way she could ever control a group of children, much less keep their attention, unless she could learn to gain access to the charismatic part of her personality that she usually kept under wraps. She knew that it was not within her means, or part of her style, to be irreverent, humorous, or dramatic the way some of her colleagues chose to entertain and interest their students. No, the one thing in life that Randi felt passionate about, in her own quiet way, was the beauty and elegance of numbers. As a math teacher, she knew that very few other people (and especially few students) felt the way she did about algebraic equations or geometric theorems. But she believed that if somehow she could communicate to her classes in a natural, authentic way her enthusiasm and excitement about mathematics, maybe some of the energy would become contagious.

Her students would sometimes notice how their usually reserved teacher seemed to come alive at certain times. Her eyes would become electric, her face would become animated. She would start pacing. Her arms would almost vibrate. Her voice would rise not so much in volume as in pitch. She became so caught up in what she was explaining, it was almost impossible not to look at her. Even with little interest in the subject or no understanding of what she was talking about, students could not help but watch her in action. It is so rare, after all, to come in contact with people who absolutely love what they do and are able to communicate this passion with abandon.

The transformation that would take place in Randi once she was in front of her classes (not all the time, not even most of the time, but enough to keep the students' attention) was, indeed, a form of charisma. She was able to use not so much her compelling personality as her passion for what she was teaching to empower her presentations. Some students could not help but wonder to themselves,

"Hey, if this quiet lady can get so worked up over these stupid numbers, maybe there is something there that I'm missing." Others would say to themselves, "I don't much care for this subject, but it sure is fun to watch her in action: It makes me want to learn this stuff."

Charisma, in whatever form it manifests itself, works to command other people's interest in what we are doing. It is not necessary to be an actor or an exhibitionist or to have a florid personality to be charismatic; but it is absolutely crucial to feel passionately about what you are doing and to be able to convey this enthusiasm to others.

Compassion

Children, and for that matter all other living creatures, appreciate people who are genuinely caring and loving toward them. This is why the best teachers are so much more than experts in their fields and more than interesting personalities—they are individuals whom children can trust, they are adults who are perceived as safe and kind and caring. Even when they are in a bad mood, give difficult assignments, or have to teach units that are relatively boring, compassionate teachers will get the benefit of the doubt from students.

When you think again about your greatest teachers, who may not necessarily have seemed like the kindest people, you still had little doubt that they had your best interests at heart. They may have pushed you, may even have shoved you hard, but you knew in your heart that they cared deeply about you as a person. You felt their respect and, yes, sometimes their love.

Very few people go into education in the first place to become rich or famous. On some level, every teacher gets a special thrill out of helping others; unfortunately, after many years in the classroom, some veterans lose the idealism that originally motivated them to be professional helpers. Yet, the teachers who flourish, those who are loved by their students and revered by their colleagues, are those who feel tremendous dedication and concern for others—not just because they are paid to do so, but because it is their nature and their ethical responsibility.

There are few rushes in life more pleasurable and fulfilling than the act of helping another human being. Some time ago, I (J. K.) was walking down the street when I came upon a group of children waiting for their school bus. Two kids, a little boy and girl of about 6 or 7 years, seemed to be involved in a tussle. As I drew closer, the girl pushed the boy down on the sidewalk, his backpack fell open, and his papers started blowing away. I reached down to retrieve the papers, helped the little boy up, and asked him if he was all right. He blinked away his tears and smiled up at me as if I were an angel. As I continued on my walk, I looked over my shoulder and saw the little boy still staring with wonder at this stranger who had rescued him.

This incident, so perfectly ordinary, seemed to transform my whole spirit. I felt so good inside I could barely restrain myself from breaking out into a whoop of exhilaration. I had helped someone who needed me. In my own tiny way, in those few seconds, I made the world a better place.

In fact, this altruistic spirit, this urge to "do good" for others, is what motivates most of us to do this sort of work (Kottler, 2000). We are driven by the desire, maybe even the need, to leave the world, or at least our little part of it, better off than before we arrived on the scene. In a sense, we become immortal in that we remain alive as long as there are others walking around this planet who were directly or indirectly helped by our compassionate efforts (Blacker, 1997).

We remember vividly the exhilaration that we have felt, and that other teachers describe, when we *know* we have made a difference in someone's life. It can involve explaining an idea that a child has never understood before. It can mean offering a smile, a hug, or a word of encouragement to someone who is suffering. It often involves reaching out in the most ordinary of circumstances to touch someone with our concern and caring. It does not take place only when we are "on duty" in the classroom. Some of the most helpful things that a teacher can ever say to a child take place in more informal settings—in the hallways, on the playground, in the lunchroom—during those times when compassion can be expressed most genuinely (Hazler, 1998).

This compassionate empathy operates not only between parents and children, between therapists and their clients, but also, most assuredly, between teachers and students. It is, in fact, the glue that binds together everything that we do in education. For unless students sense that we really value them and respect them (even as we disapprove strongly of certain ways that they may behave), there is no way that they will ever trust us and open themselves up to hear what we have to say.

You only need to examine your own significant learning experiences to understand the crucial importance that compassion plays in education. Bring to mind, once again, those teachers who have made the most difference in your life, whether a relative, a coach, a professor, a teacher, or whoever. We suggest that beyond the content of what they passed on to you, apart from their formal lessons of instruction, what you appreciated most was what genuinely caring individuals they were. They really cared about your welfare. You trusted them and learned from them because you knew they cared. Actually, that is the foundation of self-esteem; it is based on the regard that others have invested in you. How else can children learn to care about themselves and others if they do not feel such compassion and love from you, their teacher?

If you review what you believe children should receive as a result of their educational experiences, number one on your list (or certainly in the top three) would be developing a sense of self-esteem. It is from this basic attitude toward self that all confidence, competence, and life satisfaction emanates—not only during the school years but throughout a lifetime.

What is it that fosters self-esteem in children? What is it that helps young people to feel good about themselves? Among several other variables, such as mastering age-appropriate developmental tasks, developing competence in life skills, and belonging to a supportive peer group, is receiving lots of support and caring from adult mentors. It is from this position of dedicated, consistent, and compassionate caring that the effective teacher is able to set limits, create and enforce rules, establish effective classroom routines, provide discipline when it is needed—and be able to do so without risk of losing children's respect in the process.

Egalitarianism

Good teachers are certainly not mushy pushovers. Yes, they are compassionate, sometimes even permissive, but they recognize that children need and even crave having the teacher set limits. It is not so much that students despise discipline in the classroom, but rather that they will not abide rules that are unfair or that are applied indiscriminately. It is even safe to say that what children complain about the most in school are those teachers who they perceive as biased or inequitable in the ways they enforce rules. As one 10-year-old explains,

She is just so mean I hate her. You never know what to expect. There is this one girl who can get away with anything. She whispers or passes notes and Mrs. ___ just tells her to "please be quiet." But if the other kids in the class are caught doing the same thing, then she punishes them. The other day she wouldn't let anybody go outside for recess just because a few kids were making a disturbance. I wasn't even talking, but I had to stay inside, too. I just hate her.

If we consider modeling human qualities to be an important part of the teacher's role, then certainly demonstrating our own sense of fairness is crucial to helping children evolve their moral thinking. We cannot forget that teaching is an intrinsically moral act. As Weissbourd (2003) says, the moral development of students depends on the adults in their lives. How are children supposed to learn moral values, such as treating others with respect and fairness, unless they see their teachers practicing these behaviors on a daily basis?

Imagine, for example, a situation in which no matter what the teacher does on a particular day, the class is unruly and unresponsive. Cajoling, pleading, threatening, yelling, reasoning, distracting are all met with stony student resistance. The teacher knows that some decisive action is indicated, but cannot think of what it might be. From among the on the available choices, the following options are considered:

1. Pick out the ringleaders of the class disturbances and administer after school detention.

2. Announce to the class that all members are responsible not only for their own behavior but also for that of their peers. Unless the disturbances cease immediately, *they* will all suffer the same consequences regardless of their relative contributions to the problem.

3. Select the few members of the class who have been visibly identified engaging in the disruptive behavior and subject them to some form of punishment.

As is so often true in any of the behavioral sciences, determining the best and fairest solution to this problem is a judgment call. There is probably no way to predict with certainty that any of the above options is the right one, and that the others are assuredly wrong.

What is at issue here for the egalitarian teacher is not so much the action taken, but the particular way in which it is accomplished. During the moment of decision, when the teacher is immersed in the fray of classroom conflict, when confusion and frustration prevail, there is simply no time to reason through what will definitely work and what probably will not. Much of the time, the teacher is acting on instinct and experience.

It is not only unreasonable, but even impossible, for students to expect that any teacher will demonstrate perfect equity in all situations and circumstances. What children (and all of us) appreciate is the effort on the part of authority figures to do their best to understand what is going on and try to resolve the conflict with relative impartiality and objectivity. For example, after a heated exchange or conflict, the teacher has an excellent opportunity to discuss with students the process of what took place, how things got out of control, and how situations could be handled differently in the future (such reflective thinking is discussed further in a later chapter). The egalitarian teacher is not necessarily unbiased and just all of the time, but strives to be as fair as humanly possible in situations that are often impossible. Where rules are necessary, the egalitarian teaches the rules rather than simply dictating them (Jones, 1987; Powell, McLaughlin, Savage, & Zehm, 1999).

Working With Diverse Students

At the same time, teachers must address the differences in the diverse abilities of the students in their classrooms. Children with special needs require modifications of curriculum and adaptations in the classroom in order to be successful. For example, a teacher may have a student with a physical disability, a sensory impairment, learning disability, attention deficit disorder, or emotional disturbances, each requiring special attention. There will be different academic and behavioral expectations for these students according to an Individualized Education Plan (IEP). The abilities of gifted and talented students present another set of challenges (Kottler et al., 2004).

Effective teachers will implement different strategies, groupings, and assessments so that each can be successful. They differentiate the curriculum, the learning activities, and how student progress will be measured and then determine the instructional design. Students may access material through different means, such as listening to a CD, watching a DVD, or reading text. They may work individually, with a partner or in a small group or as a whole class. Finally, they may be assessed through a traditional pencil and paper test or through a form of alternative assessment, such as a product or performance. Additionally, Willard-Holt (2003) suggests curriculum compacting, tiered assignments, and multilevel learning stations will challenge all students. "Thus, students can use a variety of approaches to gain access to the curriculum, make sense of their learning, and show what they have learned" (Villa & Thousand, 2003, p. 23). In this way, all students have access to the curriculum ensuring equity. Students recognize they are all treated fairly, although not the same.

Gender Issues

The last point we want to mention relates to gender in the classroom. Research in the 1990s reported by the American Association of University Women revealed that classroom teachers treated boys and girls differently, with boys receiving more attention from teachers. Ryan and Cooper (2004) describe that boys have higher levels of participation than girls. "Boys are more likely to call out, and when they do, teachers are apt to accept the call out and continue with the class. When girls call out, a much less frequent occurrence, the teacher's typical response is to correct the inappropriate behavior" (Ryan & Cooper, 2004, p. 99). They note boys receive more criticism, praise, and feedback than girls. There are also differences in the quantity and types of advanced classes boys take when compared to girls.

While noting research reports show improvements in recent years, Ryan and Cooper suggest several measures for teachers, such as taking into account all learning styles (see Chapter 2), being aware of your interactions with your students, selecting materials that are not gender biased, choosing groups rather than letting students self select with whom they will work, and making sure all students have opportunities to participate. Calling on students rather than letting them call out answers will help to ensure fairness. Many teachers use a monitoring system, such as names on index cards drawn from a stack or names on popsicle sticks picked from a can.

Students may not comment, but they are very much aware of who participates in class and how much, as well as who is commended and how for their work. Encourage and praise all students for their work. Teachers must attend to all the students in their classes and be sensitive to how they respond to each situation from behavioral, academic, instructional, and gender perspectives.

Sense of Humor

If there is one major premise of effective teaching, it is conveying the idea that learning is enjoyable. When students are bored or uninterested, when their attention is diverted toward internal fantasies or external distractions, little learning takes place. In the marketplace of life, we are competing with a variety of other stimuli that are vying for children's attention. While sitting in the classroom, a student may be distracted by unbridled pangs of hunger, longing for peer acceptance, or lust. Compared to the worries, heartbreaks, and interests in their lives, the absolute last thing in the world that many students care about is what you are doing in class. Think about it: When children are upset about their parents fighting, or distraught because a best friend was mean, or worried about getting a part in the school play, or excited about an upcoming tennis match, just how important do *you* think whatever you are teaching is.

One principle that is crucial to keep in mind, maybe the single most important concept of education, is that nothing that is taking place in the classroom is as important to children as what they are constructing inside their own internal worlds. Ask children what they would prefer to be doing with their time, and it is likely you will get a long list of possibilities—riding bikes, talking to friends, skateboarding, eating ice cream, trading baseball cards, watching television, going to the beach, sleeping late—but quite far down on the list would be the choice, "If I could be doing anything right now, I would like to be in school, right here in *your* class."

It is our job, therefore, not only to teach children, but first to interest them in learning. A sense of humor and playfulness are among the most powerful tools available to teachers to help accomplish this mission. It is one of the ways teachers can connect with students (Wolk, 2003). Play, after all, is the language of children. It is through laughter that we all feel most enraptured, most alive, most connected to what is happening around us.

One of the most challenging teaching assignments that I (J. K.) ever faced included a group of a dozen preschoolers, ages 3 to 4 years. From the looks of their behavior, they did not appear to know the first thing about such ideas as cooperation, sharing, taking turns, or being considerate about others' feelings. I was informed that it was my job to teach them basic social skills (in addition to such life skills as mastering the use of scissors). The hardest part of my task, I soon discovered, was simply commanding their attention for long enough to teach them anything.

None of the usual things I had tried worked very well. I tried being polite (they ignored me). I switched to being unduly firm (they became afraid of me). Yet, the one thing these little people taught me that I have never forgotten is that if I could get them to laugh, they would follow me anywhere. I became so unpredictably silly in their minds, prone to do almost anything at any moment, that they were afraid if they turned their attention away for very long, they might miss something really good.

This practice of capitalizing on humor has served me well in a variety of settings. One of my teaching assignments was working with cadets at a military academy. These young men, though bright and motivated, would drag into class so utterly exhausted in the morning that they would stand up in the back of the room to avoid falling asleep (and some of them even taught themselves to sleep standing up) often worn out from the exercise regimen they began every morning at 5 a.m. after staying up all night studying.

This situation may not be that far from the one that will face you. Many children are deprived of the sleep they need to function attentively at school. They may have stayed up watching television, playing video games, talking on the phone, or surfing the Internet. They may have maintained an all-night vigil over a sick or dying pet. They may have lain awake all night as their parents battled and quarreled. They may have been up late to finish a project due that day. Whatever the cause, it is every teacher's nightmare to have to capture the attention of students who are undergoing sleep deprivation. Yet, this is the training ground for making superlative instructors. If you can keep these people awake, much less teach them anything, you are indeed in the ranks of the best.

We are not suggesting that teaching and learning are as simple as fun and games. What valuing humor means for the teacher, however, is making a commitment to appreciating the sublime, silly, playful aspects of life. It means spending as much time and attention trying to be interesting and relevant to students' needs as it does preparing the content of what we have to teach. It means acknowledging what is funny, and that funny things happen in the classroom. It also means cultivating the children's own appreciation for humor. And, yes, when appropriate, use games in the classroom. Erwin (2003) identifies review games, drama games, brain teasers, and adventure-based learning as ways to building relationships.

We promise you: If you do not encourage humor and play in class, the students will do it for you. That is the purpose of the "class clown," after all, as comedians like George Carlin and Bill Cosby have so humorously testified. When teachers fail to make learning fun, when they fail to demonstrate a sense of humor, they make for ripe targets by those creative, mischievous kids who see their job in life as helping others to have as much fun as possible.

Of the personal dimensions of teaching, humor is the most human of all. Teachers who value humor, who not only tolerate laughter and fun in their classrooms but even invite them in and encourage them to stay, are perceived by students as being more interesting and relevant than those who appear grim and humorless. A sense of humor encourages a teacher to take advantage of those "teachable moments" that serendipitously come to all classrooms. Your sense of humor will communicate to your students that you are creative, witty, subtle, and fun loving. Who else would students pay attention to and respect?

Additional Desirable Traits

The best teachers access not just what is in their heads but also what is in their hearts. They are both logical and intuitive. They are responsive both to what they observe on the outside and to what they sense on the inside. In the words of Parker Palmer (1998), "We teach who we are: I am a teacher at heart, and there are moments in the classroom when I can hardly hold the job. When my students and I discover uncharted territory to explore, when the pathway out of a thicket opens up before us, when our experience is illuminated by the lightning-life of the mind—then teaching is the finest work I know" (p. 1).

In their study of "legendary" teachers, Scheidecker and Freeman (1999) asked adults to reflect on their experiences in school and describe the characteristics of their very best teachers. It would be simple enough for you to replicate this research by doing your own interviews. In addition to the several qualities we have mentioned, you would likely discover that the following characteristics are described most frequently. As you go through this list, think about where you stand in each of these human dimensions:

- *Smarts.* This means you know stuff. You understand things that children want to know. You are perceived as being intelligent not just in "book smarts" but also in "street smarts." You are respected because of your wisdom. Children gravitate toward you because they believe that you know things that are important.
- *Creativity.* You keep students on their toes. You are unpredictable at times, playful and spontaneous. You are able to demonstrate in your own life the sort of creative spirit that you want your students to develop. Rather than overemphasizing "right" answers, you are also interested in promoting their creative behavior, especially the sort that is not disruptive and is "on task."
- *Honesty.* You can be trusted. You are not afraid to say, "I don't know," or "I'm wrong," or "I made a mistake." You model the sort of openness, transparency, and authenticity that encourage others to do the same.
- *Emotional stability.* You are relatively calm. You are not prone to the sort of mood swings or temper tantrums that make children fearful. During those times you become upset, you are able to restrain yourself so you do not lash out at kids. When you do lose control, you do what you can to make things right. You apologize. You accept responsibility for your lapse. You do not blame others. You get help for yourself. Most important, you learn from the experience so you do not do it again.
- *Patience.* Some of the worst teachers are those who are instructing in subjects that came very easy to them. It all seems so simple, and they cannot understand why others have so much trouble. Likewise, when you personally have struggled mightily to master a subject, you can more easily appreciate what others are going through. Patience often comes from this empathic understanding of what is involved in tackling what is perceived as a difficult subject. Time and time

again, students mention how important it is for their teachers to be patient with them. We cannot emphasize enough the importance of increasing "wait time" before calling on a student for an answer, of giving students a pause to reflect on what they have learned, and time to make mistakes from which they can progress.

- *Ability to challenge and motivate.* This is a complex characteristic because, on the one hand, you want to motivate students to go as far as they can but, on the other hand, you do not want to overwhelm or discourage them. If you are perceived as having both high standards and a certain flexibility, students will work hard for you, knowing that you will not compare them to others but consider their unique background and capabilities.

- *Novelty.* Another way to describe this characteristic is "differentness." Almost everyone enjoys learning experiences that are not the same as what they are used to, within certain limits. Memorable teachers seem to be those who have certain eccentricities, unique qualities, and personal idiosyncrasies that were perceived as "endearing" rather than "annoying." They also try different instructional strategies and are not afraid to take reasonable risks with new approaches.

- *Interest in students.* The revered teachers are the ones who show a genuine interest in their students. They show their school spirit by wearing school colors and participating in school events, attending assemblies, and participating in fundraising. They engage their students in conversations about their lives outside of school. They not only talk about forthcoming school and community events, they attend football games, concerts, the spring play, debates, and dances. They meet students at the door and compliment them on their extracurricular achievements. They are available before and after school to help students with homework for any class, talk about the future opportunities, and just listen to what is on their minds. They draw students' interests into their lessons showing not only that they have heard what has been said, but that it was relevant and meaningful.

In addition, the best teachers (a) are well organized and good managers, (b) hold high expectations for themselves and others, (c) are thoughtful in that they prevent classroom and discipline problems before they begin, (d) are accessible and easily approachable, and (e) are warm and empathic (Kleiner, 1998). Being a teacher means being an interesting person, someone who is wise and approachable and personally attractive.

BEING PERSONALLY EFFECTIVE

The paradox of being a great teacher is that one must be perceived not only as someone who is playful but also as someone who is efficient enough to get the job done. The job is the business of learning, which if done properly has its own intrinsic rewards. Everyone enjoys the thrill of mastering a new skill or understanding a new concept.

For teachers to be effective in the classroom, as in the world outside of school, it is necessary for them to work at being reasonably well adjusted human beings. Teachers who are ineffectual, wimpy, or whiny, who are perceived as weak and ineffective in their basic style of interaction, earn little respect from students or from their peers. Likewise, those teachers who appear to be in charge of their own lives, who radiate power, tranquility, and grace in their actions, are going to command attention and respect. Their students will follow them anywhere.

What we are saying is that you have not only the option but the imperative to develop the human dimensions of your personal functioning, as well as your professional skills. Teachers are, after all, professional communicators. We relate to others for a living. We introduce people to new ideas. We help students to build their self-esteem and confidence. We develop relationships with people to influence them in positive ways. How are we ever going to do these things unless the children we teach are attracted to us and like us as human beings?

The best teachers are those who have worked hard both to develop themselves as experts in their fields and to practice what they know and understand in their own personal lives. They are relatively free of negative emotions, and when they do become upset they have the skills to regain control. Perhaps most of all, such teachers attempt to live the ideals that they espouse to others. If they preach to others the importance of truth, honesty, self-discipline, knowledge, growth, taking constructive risks, then they practice these same values in their own lives. They become living examples for their students, showing that what they say is important enough for them to apply to their own lives. They are attractive models who advertise, by their very being, that learning does produce wondrous results.

Perhaps there are other attributes that you consider to be even more important than the teacher qualities we have identified in this chapter. These may be character traits, skills, values, cultural beliefs, or knowledge that you consider absolutely crucial to teachers who plan on making a difference in children's lives. Whatever choices you would select as being among your highest priorities to develop in yourself, the goal must remain to make yourself not only an accomplished professional but also the most effective human being you can be.

Your responsibility, then, involves so much more than presenting course content or making sure your students score high on achievement tests. The human dimensions of teaching come together in your commitment to make teaching much more than a job. Being a teacher is a way of life. You are a teacher not only when you stand in front of your classroom, but also as you walk through life, applying what you know and understand and can do.

SUGGESTED ACTIVITIES

1. Interview students at the elementary, middle, and high school levels to see who their favorite teachers are and why. Compare their answers to find common qualities.

2. Discuss with others the roles teachers have played in your lives.

3. Shadow a teacher for a day to note the variety of interactions encountered with other people. Discuss with that teacher, if possible, how the movement for standards and accountability is impacting the human dimension of teaching.

4. Read more about No Child Left Behind on the U.S. Department of Education Web site at http://www.ed.gov/nclb/landing.jhtml

CHAPTER TWO

On Being a Learner

> *Those special teachers we know, with all the personal and professional qualities we admire, share another important feature that ensures their success: They possess very clear beliefs about learning. They have an understanding about how to best customize content to fit the unique requirements of a situation and the capabilities of students. They are aware of the many obstacles to learning and know how to prevent potential problems before they occur. They know what learning is all about because they are committed, lifelong learners themselves.*

LEARNING VERSUS SCHOOLING

Too frequently, much of the professional training and practice of teachers is focused on schooling. Practitioners spend large amounts of time designing lessons; preparing bulletin boards; setting up Web pages; responding to e-mail; returning phone calls; copying seatwork; setting up and enforcing classroom rules; preparing and administering examinations; reporting absences; and readying students for photographs, assemblies, fire drills, recesses, open houses, and walking down the hall. In their classrooms, students likewise spend inordinate amounts of time copying agendas, completing worksheets; reviewing assignments; doing homework; proofreading compositions; answering the questions at the end of a chapter; and taking tests, lots of tests—achievement tests, placement tests, pretests, posttests, pop quizzes, benchmark assessments, midterms and finals. In the frenzy of these fast-paced and time-consuming activities, a critical distinction is often overlooked. How much of what occurs in school classrooms produces meaningful learning? How much is genuine learning, and how much is just schooling?

Schooling is a compulsory experience in which students are expected to acquire the knowledge and skills of the required curriculum. Schooling demands that students pay attention, listen carefully, take notes, raise their hands to ask pertinent questions, and pass the test at the end of the unit. Schooling requires students to decipher classroom rules, consequences, and routines, which may vary greatly from grade level to grade level, period to period.

Eldridge Cleaver, an African American activist of the 1960s, is a graphic example of the turned-off learner. He spent many frustrating years in classrooms before he was locked up in San Quentin prison for his violations of the law. Cleaver may have acquired the expected spelling and handwriting skills during his years of formal schooling, but he did not learn to make decisions, solve problems, and express his innermost thoughts and feelings in writing. It took the forced confinement of prison before his private voice was liberated. Locked securely behind prison bars, without the aid of teachers or textbooks, Cleaver taught himself to write. "I began to write," he recalls in his book *Soul on Ice* (1968), "in order to save myself" (p. 8).

Cleaver's experience demonstrates the critical difference between schooling and *learning*. Schooling is an "outside-in" experience. It is a necessary part of a student's education. Schooling taught him how to follow rules, take turns, play safely, and interact respectfully with teachers and peers. Learning, however, is an "inside-out" process, in which students construct an understanding of themselves, their beliefs and values, and the world in which they live. Learning is a challenging process of discovery that requires little external push; the motivation comes from within. It is the personal quest for new information, new meanings, new challenges, and experiences.

Teachers may spend too much time teaching children to follow rules and not enough on actual learning, so that we are training the next generation to be followers rather than original thinkers:

"Raise your hand if you have something to say."

"Your reports should be six pages long."

"Make sure you color between the lines."

"Mark your answers by penciling in the circle next to your choice."

"You must sharpen your pencil and be in your seat before the bell rings."

"Don't do anything disruptive—that includes fidgeting, drumming your pencil on the desk, chewing gum, throwing paper in the wastebasket, making noises, or asking questions while I am speaking."

"No talking to your neighbor. If you have something important to say, wait until *after* school is over."

Rules are certainly important for giving students guidelines for monitoring their own behaviors and for understanding the consequences of their choices. Classroom routines and procedures are also necessary for maintaining some degree of organization and order in the classroom. Chaos is no more a constructive environment for learning than is regimentation. But when the focus of teaching becomes classroom management rather than enlightenment, something is out of kilter. Many an experienced teacher would be among the first to complain, "I would love to spend time teaching instead of trying to control these children, but they have no respect for other people. They don't care about school. All they want to do is play; they don't want to work."

Well, of course they want to play! Who doesn't? But who said that learning always had to be work, that it could not be fun? One definition of work is that it is something that you *have* to do, whereas play is something that you *want* to do. "It inspires creativity and reduces stress" (Erwin, 2003, p. 22). Consider, for example, two children who are asked to police the playground for litter. The first child thinks to himself, "What a pain! Why do I always get stuck with these chores? What is this, a prison camp? I hate doing this." The second child talks to herself quite differently: "This is great. I get time to be outside and by myself. Plus, I get to do something important and help make this place cleaner. I love making up stories about how each article I find—a gum wrapper, a can, a shoelace, or a cigarette butt—ended up on the ground where I found it."

The two children are completing the exact same task, yet one views the assignment as the ultimate exercise in frustration whereas the other treats it as a fun game that gives her an opportunity to relax while accomplishing something worthwhile. If you accept this distinction (that your attitude about what you are doing is more important than the actual activity), then we should be spending a whole lot more time trying to foster positive attitudes toward school and making learning fun. This means that learning is so much more than introducing facts or presenting material. It is primarily an internal activity in which a person feels motivated to acquire new and relevant information and skills and, most importantly, enjoys the process. It is fun, not work, because the learner has reasons for mastering what is being presented.

How do you help children to *want* to learn? How do you encourage them to treat school as fun rather than work? The answer to these questions is simpler than you may imagine. Fun takes place during the following circumstances:

- When you are concentrating with all your effort and energy on a task that you have recently mastered. (Yes, that does sound suspiciously like work; the main difference is the feeling of competence in accomplishing something that you perceive to be important.)
- When you are being challenged to do something that is not beyond your ability and, when mastered, will allow you to accomplish other things that you want to do.
- When time flies because you are engaged, doing something interesting and entertaining.
- When you are talking to yourself and others about things that are relevant to your life.
- When you are interacting with *your* peers and feel understood and accepted by them.

We hope that you can see the pattern emerging here. Students love learning when the teacher makes an effort to involve them in the process of choosing what they learn about, the way in which they learn it, and when they are helped to personalize the subject in such a way that it seems useful, relevant, and important to getting them what they want in life. Erwin (2003) maintains that by building relationships based on what is internally motivating, students will be more likely to succeed.

Window Into a Classroom

Kristen is a substitute teacher. She walks into a new classroom with fear running through her arteries. She has heard about this group of children. They are unruly and disrespectful. Their regular teacher has done nothing but complain about the problems she has encountered: kids coming in late, falling asleep, talking constantly, making obscene noises, generally being downright cruel to one another and to her. Needless to say, Kristen is more than a bit apprehensive. As she enters the room, there is a brief moment of silence as the students stare momentarily at the newcomer before they return to their arguments. Kristen is determined that not only is she going to get them to settle down, but she also is going to make sure they learn something today. Maybe those two goals are related, she reminds herself.

With a confident voice, Kristen introduces herself to this notorious collection of seventh-grade boys and girls: "Good morning, class. My name is Miss Templeton, and I am here today to share something with you that I think you'll find useful and interesting."

"No, we won't!" a belligerent adolescent male bellows, knowing that he can get away with almost anything with a substitute teacher.

"Yeah? You sound pretty sure of yourself," she challenges the boy. "How can you be so certain that you won't find this interesting? I had no idea you could predict the future."

The class starts to laugh, but it is a nervous, hesitant reaction, as if students are unsure whose side they are on.

"Because we never get to do anything fun in this class," the boy yells back, looking around him to make sure that others are still in support. "Besides," he offers as an afterthought, "social studies is dumb!"

"What could make social studies fun for you?" Kristen asks, mostly stalling for time until she can locate his name on the teacher's seating chart. She finds the name "Amy" listed and realizes that they are playing the "switching names and seats" game.

"Let's talk about the stuff we're really interested in instead of the teacher always talking at us," continues the disgruntled youth in Amy's seat.

"You must be a mind reader after all," Kristen quickly replies, "because that's *exactly* what I have planned for you today!"

Kristen moved so quickly in rearranging the desks into six groups of five students that they did not have time to level any further protests. She then shared a brief story about teenage friends, Heather and Tina, who spend time together in and out of school. One day, Tina discovers that she has a problem. Her trusted friend, Heather, has cheated her out of some of her hard-earned money and has used it to buy a new pair of sunglasses.

Kristen gives each group 15 minutes to come up with a solution to Tina's problem. The room begins to buzz as the members of the groups discuss the problem and suggest solutions. From time to time, one of the groups erupts with laughter about one of their off-the-wall suggested solutions. Kristen is surprised to observe that these explosions of laughter do not interfere with the group's ability to complete the task. In fact, the spontaneous laughter appears to help the students deal with difficult decisions and differences of opinion. She gives the groups a warning that they have 5 minutes left to come up with a solution to share with the whole class.

"Time is up. Move your desks back where they were so we can share our solutions to Tina's problem . . . and class . . . this time I want you to sit in your assigned seats." They smile in recognition that they have been found out.

The remainder of the class period is spent in an animated sharing and comparing of solutions. After each group reveals its unique solution, embellished in an imaginative teenage way, Kristen skillfully leads the students to consider the consequences of their proposed ideas and to reconsider the appropriateness of their original solution. Suddenly, the bell rings, surprising the students, who had lost themselves in this interesting class. As they file out, the belligerent male student furtively passes Kristen a note written on a corner of a piece of notebook paper. It says, "Your class was fun. I have a brother who cheats me all the time. I got some ideas today about how to make him stop messing with me. Thanks."

This window into a classroom demonstrates one way that learning can be fun, interesting, amusing, punctuated with laughter, and still reach its intended outcomes. An overemphasis on schooling, however, frequently results in students who either become teacher pleasers, passively going through the motions, or become turned off, frustrated learners often labeled with some learning disability.

Both kinds of students frequently find themselves *managed* by teachers in classrooms with more worksheets and quiet assignments of "read the chapter and answer the ten questions at the end." Is it surprising that many students find this *type* of schooling an abysmal waste of their time?

How People Learn

As you grow into the kind of teacher *you* want to be, you will find it helpful to view learning theories not as didactic sets of rules for teaching but as tools to help you better understand your teaching and your students' learning (see, for example, Bigge & Shermis, 1998; Brooks & Brooks, 1999; Schunk, 1999). In other courses and studies, you will learn about various approaches to learning with names like "constructivist," "cognitive," "behavioral," "humanistic," and so on. You will also likely experience a fair degree of confusion, as each theory seems to contradict the others.

In spite of their significant differences, most approaches to learning take into consideration the following factors:

Learning Variables

There are certain factors that are most often associated with learning, especially the kind that sticks with students over time:

- The teaching relationship and the connections you are able to create with students such that they feel valued and respected
- The cognitive activity that takes place internally in which students personalize content in light of their language, background, culture, and experience
- The consequences and reinforcements of behaviors that are rewarded and others that are punished
- The opportunities for practicing and rehearsing new skills and behaviors, with constructive feedback to improve performance
- Cooperative and interactive experiences that allow students to work together to solve problems and apply what is being learned, as well as to express their ideas
- Challenges to their current perspective or functioning that force students to develop alternative points of view or strategies
- Introduction to novel ideas and stimulating, enriched environments
- Modeling of effective behaviors

Although hardly exhaustive, this list gives you some idea of the relatively generic variables that are often associated with constructive learning processes. The more you observe students as they question, examine, explore, and analyze their world, the more you will discover ways to develop your own methods to encourage their meaning-making efforts.

Constructivism

Many successful instructional approaches in the contemporary curriculum areas of mathematics, science, language arts, and social studies are being built upon the social and cognitive constructivists' views of teaching and learning (Anderson, 1984; Henderson, 1996; Hewson & Hewson, 1988; Marlowe & Page, 1998; Saunders, 1992). Wolk (2003) adds to the discussion with his description of democratic classrooms as constructive and generative. "Democratic classrooms honor the knowledge and experiences that students bring to school and advocate learning as a social act" (Wolk, 2003, p. 17). Through personal and social experiences, students are actively involved in constructing their own learning.

According to this constructivist view, students are not viewed as blank tapes to be filled up with the knowledge from a lecturing teacher. Rather, students are engaged in the active process of building on what they already know and can do. In mathematics, students in elementary grades can create original algorithms for solving computational problems; they can generate probabilities when collecting data from their own experiments. In science, students can use their past experiences to make predictions about what will happen when different objects are submerged in liquids. They can then formulate their own theories to explain their predictions. Students in language arts class can conduct in-class polls regarding students' preferences for hot lunches, political candidates, and classroom rules. After they analyze the data they have collected, they can use this information to write real letters to the principal, the school cook, or the editor of the local newspaper to express their views, backed up by the data from their polls.

These students are actively using their language and thinking skills to construct their understanding of the world and the events that take place in it. Constructivist teachers learn to become unobtrusive during strategic times in their classrooms, subtly guiding students in the process of making connections and finding new levels of understanding and appreciation.

We recommend that you consciously study theories of learning in order to create and build on your own model that is consistent with your philosophy, values, training, and student needs. As you study the various approaches, remember that the most important theory of learning is the one you are beginning to construct for yourself. It is your current explanation of how people, including you, learn best.

Learning Styles

Students also vary in their learning styles. A mismatch between how information is presented and how students best receive and process it can lead to problems in the classroom where both the teacher and students experience frustration. Teachers need to recognize their students' learning styles and use specific, instructional strategies to address them. A brief overview of four learning styles is presented here.

- Sensory modalities: Visual learners gain knowledge best by seeing new information; auditory learners take in new information best by hearing it; kinesthetic learners like to touch and manipulate objects. Although it takes time to gather and develop resources, a teacher who uses pictures, charts, graphic organizers, and text as well as video, direct instruction, and verbal descriptions, along with artifacts, models, and acting out concepts would, indeed, provide a sensory rich environment for students.
- Global or analytic information processing: Global learners move from an understanding of the whole to the contributions of the parts focusing on spatial and relational processing; analytic learners move from the part to the whole using details to build understanding. Although students use both types of processing, they typically have a preference of one over the other. Strategies for teachers include modeling and providing practice experiences for students in both types of processing.
- Field independent or field dependent: Field independent students prefer to work alone and receive recognition for their individual endeavors; field dependent students like to work with others and look to the teacher for direction. To address both domains, teachers need to offer both self-directed, individual projects and collaborative, cooperative activities.
- Impulsive or reflective: Impulsive students are quick to give responses without much thinking and often guess at answers;

reflective students take their time before replying to avoid mistakes. Teachers need to provide opportunities for students to both make on-the-spot predictions and to wait before calling out an answer so as to give all children a chance to formulate a response.

Although it takes time to get to know your students and analyze the learning styles of the students, if you do, you will be rewarded with the relationships you build with your students and their accomplishments. Although they need to have experiences in all learning styles, they will learn and remember more when working in a style that best fits their abilities and preferences.

Multiple Intelligences

Ryan and Cooper (2004) note that schools today favor students with linguistic and analytic capabilities, especially those that can be measured on standardized tests. These children do very well in school, while other students who may even be gifted in a nontraditional area, may find their days in school frustrating and limiting, often marked by failure. Howard Gardner (1999) identified eight categories of intelligence that are widely discussed in schools and suggests we nurture all the multiple intelligences, which include existential intelligence and spiritual intelligence.

1. Verbal/linguistic—the ability to form thoughts and use language for expression

2. Spatial/visual—the ability to judge space in relation to people and/or other objects

3. Musical/rhythmic—the ability to create patterns of sound

4. Intrapersonal—the ability to think about thinking, to reflect and self-assess

5. Bodily/kinesthetic—the ability to move skillfully and manipulate objects

6. Naturalistic—the ability to understand the natural world, flora and fauna, and navigate in the environment

7. Interpersonal—the ability to communicate with others

8. Logical/mathematical—the ability to discern logical or numeric patterns

Teachers need to move beyond the first and last intelligence in working with students. There is no shortage of reading and writing assignments or small group discussion for verbal/linguistic learners. Logical/mathematical learners get plenty of challenge analyzing patterns, finding sequences, categorizing information, and exploring cause-effect relationships.

Delivery, practice, and assessments should take into account the possibilities of the other six categories as well. For example, for the spatial/visual learner, bring in pictures and artifacts, perform demonstrations, have students create drawings to show what they have learned. To honor those with musical/rhythmic intelligence and expand that area for others, teachers can use jingles, chants, and songs to introduce new information and help students with retention of information. Students can put on musical performances. To target intrapersonal intelligence, have students create journals in which they self-assess their learning. To reach bodily/kinesthetic students, have students build models, create and perform skits, or engage in simulations. Naturalistic intelligent students will flourish in working with plants and animals in the classroom. Allow them to explore the natural environment. To foster interpersonal intelligence, involve students in cooperative learning groups in which they must solve a problem.

The whole idea is that learning takes place on multiple dimensions and levels. The more different modalities that you can engage in a student's experience, the more likely that *some* facet of the lesson is going to stick.

RELEVANCE IN EDUCATION

All children, from the most dedicated honors student to the most belligerent discipline problem, want to learn. The principal challenge in education is not at all a matter of convincing our consumers that our product is worthwhile; rather, it is teaching subjects that they perceive as relevant and useful to them. Although we cannot always make all aspects of *schooling* relevant to students, we make their *learning* more relevant to their lives.

Cultural Backgrounds

We need to know who the students are in our classrooms—their personal experiences and their cultures. What are the ethnic and cultural backgrounds of our students? This includes not only race, but family values, traditions, religion, and even gender roles (Kottler et al., 2004). How students and their parents behave and interact with others in the classroom often reflects their culture. Do students look adults in the eye or look down out of respect when they talk to an adult? Do students answer "yes" to every question in order to please the adult? Do students ask questions, or are they passive in the classroom? Students will come from different socioeconomic levels as well. Those from higher levels are likely to have stronger academic backgrounds and more family support for education. How long have the students been in this country? What was their reason or their families' reason for coming? How proficient is their English? Knowledge of your students' upbringing is vital to understanding how to best make the students feel comfortable, meet their needs, and avoid miscommunication (Kottler & Kottler, 2002).

Ben-Yosef (2003) points out the importance of beginning with the cultural literacy of students, local and vernacular, by exploring the local community and having students bring examples into the classroom to use. Another common activity is to have students create their own "coat of arms" representing their friends, families, interests, and achievements. You might also consider having students create personal scrapbooks, write autobiographies, develop illustrated and annotated personal timelines, or put up a bulletin board about their community. Watching the body language of students and paying attention to what they say and when they speak will provide you with needed insight. Talk individually with students and conduct surveys for additional information. The more you know about them, the more effective you will be in your relationships. You will want to connect with them on a level that is meaningful and in a way that is personal.

English Learners

The student body in the school district where I (E. K.) work reflects the ethnically diverse and multilingual community at large. Students speak over 50 languages other than English at home.

Students are tested when they register for school for their English proficiency and placed in the appropriate English development classes. Teachers implement Specially Designed Academic Instruction in English (SDAIE) or other sheltered English strategies and work with bilingual aides when they are available. Funds are used to provide written and oral translation for parents, and support classes are offered for parents to develop skills, techniques, and strategies to help their children at home.

You may have just a few children with limited English proficiency or many in your classroom. Miller and Endo (2004) point out that schools vary widely in the types of programs they offer to support children with limited English proficiency. Some schools offer no special programs while others teach English as a second language classes or offer bilingual programs. The authors suggest the following practices for teachers with students in mainstream classrooms:

- Select activities that the students will relate to, being cognizant of their prior life experiences.
- Help students feel comfortable in the environment by giving clear directions, recognizing that their previous schooling may have required only passive behavior on the part of the student.
- Build an individual relationship with students and parents, beginning by learning how to pronounce their names in their native languages.
- Use English skillfully by simplifying complex text and speech and using language strategically with attention to specific vocabulary. Model academic language with the use of pictures and objects for additional support.
- Allow students to use their native language as they learn English while emphasizing the importance of English.
- Develop relationships with parents to monitor their children's experience as they learn English and the components of American culture.

Social Backgrounds

Finally, no matter where children are from, they come to school with a variety of social backgrounds. As Armstrong, Hensen, and Savage (2005) report, some children come from supportive homes—even the "typical" family of an employed father, a stay-at-home mother, and two siblings, though they report that less than a quarter of students actually live with both parents. Students face a variety of social problems from homelessness to poverty, family changes of birth, death, divorce, frequent moves, violence in the streets, and even violence in the home. Sometimes students make choices that result in drug and alcohol use, gang involvement, pregnancy or fathering a child, or delinquency.

As teachers, we can recognize these pressures and others, such as depression and suicide potential, and intervene to help these children. We identify the family, income, family education, ability to speak English, and other factors that place children at risk for failure in school. Additionally, are recognize and report physical, emotional, and sexual abuse as well as neglect. Using clear learning objectives with a variety of teaching strategies and monitoring their progress will help these children.

What Students Want

Providing relevant learning experiences is one of the key features of effective classrooms. (Wolk, 2003). But do not take our word for it: Listen to the voices of students. The following pleas for relevance in classroom learning experiences will not be too dissimilar from those of your own students.

Ask elementary schoolchildren what they most want to learn about, and they will tell you quite openly:

> As a 10-year-old boy, I don't like learning about periods and question marks and multiplication problems and stuff like that. I like learning about things that are more interesting. For example, when I'm playing computer games, and I press the button to make a figure on the screen jump, how does that work? All the information goes through one little wire from the joy-stick to the power box. But what happens after the information goes there?
>
> Drugs are something else I wouldn't mind knowing about. Where do they come from? How are they made? If they are supposed to be so bad for you, how come some people say they feel so good?
>
> I've got a whole long list of other things I wish we could learn about in school instead of the boring stuff we have to

study. How can I dribble the basketball better with my other hand? How can I get my mom to let me stay up later at night? How can I have more friends sleep over? How can I get my older sister to stop bothering me? How can I make some money so my parents don't have to work so hard and could come home early? How do I prove myself to other people? I would love to know the answers to these questions.

A middle school child is asked the same question: "What would you like to learn in school?" She responds instantly, as if she has been thinking about that very question her whole life:

I wish the teachers would just not talk so much and let us have more time to read. I wish we could go to any class we want. I want to learn about how to do magic tricks and play the piano better and have more friends. I wonder why people don't melt and why donuts have holes in them. I would like to learn how to work a compass and find my way back home if I got lost.

A high school student answers the question with equal fluency:

I would really like to understand what I can do to get girls to like me. I wish I could figure out what they really want. I want to know a whole lot more about love and sex. First of all, how do I get someone to have sex with me, and, second, what is most important to girls about it? I would like to know how to have more friends and be more popular. I wish I could learn how to get my parents to stop fighting. I want to know what I'm going to do when I get out of this place—how I'm going to find a good job. I would love to learn more about fixing cars. I've got this transmission problem, the gears are always slipping.

As these three typical children have testified, there is indeed no shortage of things that almost anyone would like to learn about. The problem, however, is that we are mandated to teach subject areas that have not been selected by our consumers, but rather by their guardians. So when we teach math and history and handwriting and grammar and economics, we must explain why they are included in the curriculum, why they are important. Furthermore, as mentioned earlier, teachers are under increasing pressure to improve performance on basic competency tests, reducing degrees of freedom even more.

Did anyone ever explain to you why you spent endless tedious hours learning to diagram sentences? To this day, can you tell the difference between a subject and predicate? Did any teacher ever sufficiently convince you of the value of proving geometric theorems or balancing algebraic equations? Did you ever stand at the blackboard, chalk in hand, utterly befuddled—not only as to how to do what the teacher asked but, more importantly, as to why you should invest any energy in learning to do so? Did you ever wonder why we bothered to learn math with all the memorizing of times tables and completing of pages of long division problems, especially because there are computers and calculators to serve those functions? It is not until much later that many of us realized that math is the basis of logic and problem solving and finally appreciated its relevance.

What can be seen from reading these examples of what children want to learn in school is that there is a gigantic discrepancy between their interests and what they actually spend their time studying.

Another problem has to do with the implicit but unintended messages that children pick up during their educational career. What is it that children really learn in school? According to John Holt (1968), they receive these messages:

- Learning is not what is most important; getting good grades is, pleasing the teacher is. Staying out of trouble is what counts.
- They should feel humiliated, frustrated, and stupid when they do not know the answer to a question. When they do not know or understand something, they should keep their mouths shut.
- They should not get caught cheating; but if they can get away with it, they will not only save themselves time and improve performance, but they will beat the teacher at his or her own game.
- They should blend in and not make waves or create disturbances.
- Only the teacher says things that are worth remembering; nobody ever takes notes on what another student says—it will not be on the exam.
- There are such things as right answers, even if they do not exist outside the classroom.
- It is winning that counts, definitely *not* how you play the game.

- You should not work to satisfy yourself but to please others.
- School is a prison, learning is boring, and education is a drag.

These negative attitudes can and must be addressed and coun-teracted if meaningful learning is to take place. The key is to make certain that what you are teaching and how you are teaching it is perceived by learners as being relevant to their lives and helpful to reaching their personal goals.

TEACHER-RELATED OBSTACLES TO LEARNING

For a teacher, it is important to understand not only how learning takes place but also what may impede or block it. Sometimes these obstacles create temporary barriers to student learning; sometimes the barriers are permanent.

Coercion and threats, all too common in our schools, are major barriers to student learning. Glasser (1998) maintains that coercive elements, whether in the form of grades, tests, or censures, are the single greatest impediments to creating high-quality education. Hart (1983) also contends that classroom threats "downshift" the brain, rendering students virtually incapable of learning. He even suggests that feeling threatened is a common symptom experienced by many children who are identified as learning disabled. Erwin (2003) adds that perceived threats create stress resulting in negative effects—children acting out or withdrawing.

It should not be too difficult for you to draw on your own expe-riences as a student to confirm these statements. How well do you do in your classes during those times when it feels as if a threatening, critical authority figure is waiting to pounce on your every mistake? The problem is even worse when you feel, as we often do, that essen-tially you are a fraud, and if you really reveal yourself, others will find out and reject you.

Shame is a cousin of coercion and also reduces the likelihood of learning. The "shame on you" taunts of parents, teachers, siblings, and peers often result in diminishing the self-esteem of students. Without self-confidence, many students experience chronic school failures. These disappointments, in turn, beget more shame. "When a child becomes a failure in school, it is not long before there is an association with being a failure as a person" (Bradshaw, 1990, p. 61).

Fear of shame frequently results in teacher-pleasing behaviors that have little to do with meaningful learning (Powell, Zehm, & Kottler, 1995). High achievers seek to do perfect schoolwork to avoid being embarrassed by teachers or parents. They attempt to avoid failure at all costs because they feel their very survival is at stake. One of your main challenges as a teacher will be to both provide your students with opportunities for success in their learning efforts and assist them in coping with failure. In taking risks, in venturing into the unknown, in experimenting with new skills or ideas, it is inevitable that human performance will fall short of high expectations. Depending on how children deal with their mistakes, misjudgments, and imperfections, they will either become creative problem solvers and fearless truth seekers or, all too commonly, cautious academic achievers who become obsessed with grades and the approval of others. Unfortunately, this is one lesson in life that is all too often generalized to other areas.

In many classrooms for the so-called gifted and talented, another obstacle to learning may be found in the form of a competitive atmosphere. These budding scholars feel driven (or are driven by others) to succeed at all costs. They will accept no grade less than an A. Their teachers encourage them always to "strive to be the best."

Well intentioned as the competitive learning climate and slogans of excellence may be, they are often translated in students' minds as, "Do not try anything unless you are certain you can do it well, and preferably better than anyone else." If learning is measured in terms of grade point averages and standardized test scores, these students may be considered academic superstars. Unfortunately, these same students are often rigidly conventional in their thinking, afraid of taking risks, interpersonally insensitive, and emotionally immature (Getzels & Jackson, 1962; Horowitz & O'Brien, 1985).

Contrast this learning environment with remedial classrooms composed of "low-ability" or "brain-dead" students or "losers" as they are described by their peers. These children feel they have nothing to lose. They could not care less about the threat of F grades as motivators to learning. They have endured so much custodial teaching (the stay-in-your-seat, fill-in-the-blanks, and keep-quiet mode of teaching) that only one strategy can motivate them to learn: providing them with something significant and important to them as people.

In one such self-contained class of seventh-grade, low-ability students, these often-belligerent students walked into their fourth period class as I (S. Z.) was putting away some new video camera equipment provided for my third-period academically talented class. "How come we never get to make movies, Mr. Z., ain't we gifted students, too?"

"You know I think you've all got lots of smarts," I responded with obvious embarrassment, "but I'm not allowed to use the equipment with this class. Now, let's work on our spelling lists today."

The next day at the beginning of fourth period, I was dumbfounded when the students proudly pranced into my classroom with two video cameras and a bag filled with videotape cassettes. "You ain't got no excuse now, Mr. Z.," they confidently proclaimed. "We want to make our own movies now."

During the course of the following month, these students, largely written off by the system, produced a high-quality video on a theme about which they were experts. "We want to make a movie about all the hassles we got. . . . everybody hassles us!" That is exactly what they did. They were motivated to improve their reading so that they could follow the video camera instruction books. They wrote and revised their script over and over until it said exactly what they wanted it to say. These students made many mistakes, learned from them, and did what the experts in Hollywood did: They made as many retakes as they needed until they were satisfied with a particular scene or piece of dialogue.

My so-called gifted students were not so successful. They were unable to take the risks needed to be successful. Their fear of failure compelled them to shadow me, seeking my approval. "Is this right, Mr. Zehm? Did I do this the right way?" I came to realize that many of my academically talented students were high achievers whose academic work was permeated with fear of failure, fear of getting any grade lower than A. These students needed help taking academic risks on their own.

BELIEFS ABOUT LEARNING

In reading these case examples, you are likely formulating your own ideas about what leads some children to do well in school and others to fail miserably. It is a good idea to monitor continuously your beliefs about learning. Make a habit of conducting this inventory frequently. Ask yourself, "What do I believe about learning? . . . about how children mature? . . . about my lifelong growth?" Unexamined beliefs about how children learn often result in unintended, accidental, and incidental learning outcomes.

Suppose that you routinely assign fill-in-the-blanks assignments for seatwork. Your intended outcome for the language arts lesson using this exercise is the understanding of the parts of a business letter. Some weeks later, when you ask your students actually to write a business letter, you are surprised to find that most of *your* students cannot compose one with the appropriate components you thought they had "mastered" with the seatwork assignments. If you examined your beliefs about learning, you would probably agree that filling in the blanks often results in mindless, passive, compliant students. People rarely learn much from such deadening experiences.

Consider your own ideas about the optimal ways that learning takes place. Write them down in a journal. Review your list periodically. Add new understandings of how students learn as you continue to evolve. Modify or eliminate those beliefs about learning you cannot substantiate with actual classroom testing or research support. Do not forget to examine your beliefs about how you continue to grow as a learner.

The list that follows is an example of one teacher's beliefs about learning. It is intended as a guide.

My Beliefs About Learning

- I believe that all of my students are curious, natural learners.
- I believe that all of my students are capable of learning.
- I believe that my students learn best when I actively involve them in relevant learning.
- I believe that my students learn best when I provide them with a safe and stimulating learning environment.
- I believe that my students learn best when I involve them in significant learning experiences that are as close to "real life" as I can get them.
- I believe that learning is personal, so I frequently get out of the way to encourage their authentic, personal responses.
- I believe that learning is social, so I provide lots of opportunity for students to work together in cooperative groups.
- I believe that language is central to thinking and learning, so I invite my students to actively participate in a classroom alive with opportunities to read, write, talk, listen, and share.

- I believe that modeling is a powerful tool for learning, so I continue to grow personally and professionally as an enthusiastic lifelong learner.

It should now be clear to you that learning is a process that is not at all synonymous with many activities that take place in school. Although there are many different conceptions that explain how learning occurs, most agree on the importance of making the experience as dynamic and relevant as possible.

SUGGESTED ACTIVITIES

1. Review the list of beliefs about learning mentioned earlier and brainstorm how you would translate those ideas into action.

2. Interview a master teacher about creating a positive classroom environment. Inquire as to how rules are formed, what and how routines are implemented, how respect is established, and how positive relationships are built.

3. Discuss with others how to provide relevant learning experiences for students. Identify strategies you would use and resources you would need.

4. Survey students to find out what their current interests are and what they would like to learn in school.

CHAPTER THREE

On Being a Relationship Specialist

Think about your favorite teachers. Do you remember how they made you feel? How were they able to connect with you? Did you feel like those teachers really paid attention to you and made you feel special? Did you feel like the teachers really listened to you when you spoke? How did that happen? Was it what the teachers said? The language that was used? The way they looked at you? Effective teachers are specialists in building relationships.

Barbara is a high school Spanish teacher. As one of the newer members of the staff, though by no means the youngest, she is assigned to teach the introductory language courses—sections that are required for high school graduation for sophomores at her school. Many of these young men and women are not particularly interested in learning the language that Barbara has devoted her professional life to studying. Except for the minority who hope and plan to go to college, the rest of the students rarely do any homework or study for any exams.

Although the vast majority of the kids do not like studying Spanish, they do like and respect their teacher. They say she seems to be a nice enough lady, and she seems to care about them. She stays after class to talk to them. She makes an effort to get to know each of them. She even tells them things about her own life, and she is friendly when she talks to them.

When Wendy got pregnant, Kyle was kicked out of the house, and Mick came to school with a broken nose, Barbara was the first adult they could think of to talk to. She always listened to students without judging them or telling them what to do; instead she tried to be supportive and to help them to figure out things for themselves. Most importantly, they trusted her. When she suggested seeing the guidance counselor or having their parents come in for a conference, they might not do it, but at least they would listen.

Word eventually got out that Barbara was "all right." She might teach Spanish, and she might be a tough disciplinarian, but class sometimes could be fun. Her students, when questioned as to what they liked most about her, would unhesitatingly mention that they felt close to her. At basketball games or school concerts, she was among the first people that students would seek out to greet.

She acknowledges she has quite a following in the school, and she attributes it to a single factor—the time and effort she spends getting to know each and every one of the kids who will let her get close to them. It is her relationship with the students that she feels is the essence of her teaching approach.

As Barbara clearly demonstrates, it is in our relationships with children that we earn their trust. Once they have decided that we are adults worthy of their respect, they will follow us wherever we might wish to lead them, from the Peloponnesian Wars, Pythagorean theorem, and past participle to Picasso, Plato, and Pizarro. Most children couldn't care less *what* we teach as long as they feel connected to us in some intimate way.

STUDENT PERCEPTIONS OF CARING RELATIONSHIPS

One of the most important facets of effective teaching relationships is providing support and regard for students. Mendes (2003) writes that students need structure and nurture. They respond to people who care. As mentioned in the previous example, students are even willing to do work that they do not value if they feel that the teacher really cares about them.

What do students consider important in the caring relationships their teachers establish with them? In a study of the perceptions of middle grade students, Alder and Moulton (1998) reported that the perceptions of these students revealed several themes related to caring relationships, some of which may surprise you. First, students revealed that teachers demonstrate their caring when they are in control of the class. They saw the teacher's ability to take charge of the class and maintain an orderly, safe, and inviting climate as evidence of compassion and concern.

Second, students considered equal treatment of students to be an important element of teacher caring. Although we listed this in the first chapter as the personal quality of being fair, it is worth mentioning again in this context. One special education student, mainstreamed into a regular classroom, described her appreciation of the equal treatment her teacher gave her: "I don't like the yelling part, but he yells at me like a regular kid" (Adler & Moulton, 1998, p. 22).

The third perception of students revealed by the study was that they attributed caring to teachers who were able to forgive students for their mistakes. These teachers gave students the benefit of the doubt and provided second chances when appropriate. They may have had high standards, but they were also viewed as realistic and forgiving.

Students also recognized teachers as caring when the teachers genuinely expressed concern for them. This was especially the case when teachers extended themselves in some way, such as by offering encouragement and support during difficult times. They showed an interest not only in the students' schoolwork, but in their personal lives. They remembered things about students that were important, rarely failing to follow up on previous conversations.

"So, Guillermo," a second-grade teacher says in greeting one of his students as he walks into school. "I see you're here early this morning. That must mean it was a tough night last night with all your cousins visiting. Bet you couldn't wait to get out of there as soon as you could?" The little boy nods shyly, but smiles in appreciation for being recognized.

Mrs. Wilkes is sitting at her desk as her fourth-hour sophomore English class files in just under the last bell. As one girl quickly slips by her desk, the teacher remarks to her, "Good game last night. I saw you scored a goal and got two assists." The teacher knows that it is a big deal to this student to be starting on the varsity soccer team, especially because it is about the only area of her life that is currently going well.

"Thank you, ma'am," she says, half with pride and half with embarrassment. She rolls her eyes as she looks toward her friends, but she is more than a little pleased that her teacher noticed how well she was doing, especially since she was struggling so hard in this English class.

In each of these two cases, simple remarks communicated to the students that the teachers cared enough about them to remember what was most important to them. Of course, this is not enough, but it is a good foundation for everything else you do.

Finally, students revealed that a strong dimension of teacher caring was related to the quality of their teaching. They recognized a caring teacher as one who makes learning interesting and understandable, relevant and engaging. They also felt caring teachers refrained from embarrassing students publicly in front of the whole class.

HUMAN DIMENSIONS OF HELPFUL RELATIONSHIPS

Human beings were designed to function in tribes, small, intimate groups that worked and lived together in mutual cooperation (Glantz & Pearce, 1989). Each of us had dozens of caregivers, because all adults parented and mentored all the children of the tribe. The education of the children was the responsibility of the elders, who taught us to hunt and forage and to take care of ourselves and everyone else. Every member of our society developed strong interconnected bonds; we depended on one another to survive.

Now, the tribes have been disbanded. Our relatives and childhood friends are scattered across the continent. We live miles from where we were born. Children are now taught by strangers called "teachers" and taken care of by guardians called "baby-sitters." Rather than having face-to-face contact, with all the accompanying visual cues and "felt sense" of physical proximity, we are now spending more and more time developing relationships through computer screens and cell phones.

It is the warmth and nurture of human relationships that we all long for and that children most easily respond to. Learning most easily takes place in the context of a safe environment in which people feel secure enough to experiment, to take risks, to venture beyond their capabilities into the great unknown. Teachers who consistently respond with genuine warmth will, in the long run, be able to salvage rocky relationships with most belligerent students (Jones, 1987; Kottler, 2002). The relationships that we develop with children are the foundation of this learning environment, alliances that have certain definable characteristics.

Foremost, helping relationships are trusting. Moustakas (1986) describes the essence of this trust as having three facets of what it means to be close to another: *being in, being for,* and *being with.* The first dimension, *being in,* refers to what we think of as pure empathy—that is, the capacity to enter into other people's worlds, to walk around in their shoes and sense what their experiences feel like. All of us can recall instances when we have been in deep communication with someone else who we just know understands what we are talking about. We do not feel judged or criticized; we feel almost enveloped in the other person's compassion and caring for us, the deep commitment to use all powers of concentration in the effort to understand what we are experiencing.

Being for means being an advocate for someone, standing in that person's corner to offer support and nurture. This occurs when we have been able to communicate to children effectively that we are on their side, that we care deeply about them, and that we will do everything in our power to help them. Children appreciate this advocacy most of all, and when they can sense that we are their allies, they will be much more inclined to open up to us, to cooperate with the educational program, and to work hard on their own growth. It is much easier to try new things when we know that somebody we trust is waiting in the wings to catch us if we fall—somebody who will never make fun of our mistakes.

The third component of trust in helping relationships, *being with,* signifies being fully engaged with the learner but also acknowledges our separateness from this other person. *Being with* describes the clear boundaries of our relationship; we are the teachers, they are the students. A new teacher, for example, is spending huge amounts of his time worrying about some of his kids who come from poor neighborhoods: "They have nothing!" he says with despair. "What can I possibly do for them? How can I teach them when I know they are hungry, when they can't even find any decent shoes to wear?"

Although this teacher's caring and compassion are admirable, he has actually lost the boundaries between himself and those he is teaching. He is concentrating so hard on "being in" and "being for" that he has forgotten the importance of also being *with* them. That means holding their hands as much as possible, doing what you can, but also accepting the limits of what you cannot do. Otherwise, you will become so discouraged you cannot help anyone much, and you certainly will not help yourself.

When I (J. K.) was first learning to be a teacher, I took almost every kid home with me in my head. I worried about each of them. I castigated myself for not trying harder. I thought over and over again about my mistakes and misjudgments. But most of all, I spent so much spare time worrying about what the kids were doing and how they were getting along.

"How is that helping them?" my supervisor asked me, in a voice that was almost critical, I was shocked by his response. Here I thought I was going to get the martyr of the year award for caring so much.

When he saw my quizzical, hurt look, he continued, "I asked you what the connection was between you worrying about these kids and it being in any way helpful to them. When you stay up late at night, thinking about some student who is failing or having trouble at home, does it make a difference to them?"

"Ah, no," I said, still confused. "But how can I not think about them?" I continued, more than a little defensively.

"If worrying about your students isn't helping them, then what's it doing for you?"

Oops. He got me. As we continued this dialogue, what I realized is that all the worrying I was doing, all the collapse of boundaries between my professional and personal life, was really more about me than it was about my students. Certainly, concern and planning are useful, but worrying is essentially wasted energy, at least as far as helping anyone else. But what I realized is that all my obsessive activity was really a good distraction so I did not have to deal with some stuff in my own life. As long as I was so concerned with my students I did not have to think about myself.

The object lesson from this story is not that you should not think about and be concerned about your students; nor is it that you should not spend time planning strategies about how to help them better and how to improve your skills in a number of areas. Rather, it is a reminder that helping relationships also have their limits. There is only so much you can do; the rest is up to others. If you do not learn this lesson relatively quickly, you will burn yourself out in no time or, even worse, never have much of a life outside your job.

AUTHENTIC RELATIONSHIPS

To be with someone, we must not only feel empathy toward the person and be that person's advocate, but we must also be authentic and genuine in the encounter. That means that trust is reciprocal, in the sense that we also risk being ourselves in the relationship, sometimes even being vulnerable in our interactions.

For example, a fifth-grade science teacher is doing everything that he can think of to maintain his students' interest and attention on a particularly difficult day. Whatever mysterious force in the universe that controls children's behavior has conspired to energize these children so that they are unruly and unmanageable. They are throwing things across the room, ignoring the teacher's threats, pleadings, and censures. Finally, in exasperation, the teacher starts talking to them in a quiet voice about what it feels like to be him at that moment:

> You know, it is at times like this that I wonder why I do this for a living. All year long, I have been working so hard to teach you the things about science that *you* wanted to learn. You wanted to know about snakes, so I brought in snakes. You wanted to go on field trips, so I organized an expedition every month. I stay after school so I can talk with you. I call your parents when you are having a hard time. You come to me and confide your problems and I listen to you.
>
> What about me? When some of you treat me like this, and show such disrespect for me, I wonder why I put myself out so much for you. I feel hurt, and I feel angry. I would really like to hear what you think and feel about what I just said.

This is a teacher who has already established a degree of trust in his relationships with students. What it means to truly *be with others* is that it is safe to tell one another what is going on inside, knowing that each party is committed to working things out. Now, the strategy just described is not one that we are necessarily advocating for beginners to try in their classrooms; in some situations this could be perceived as weakness, and the teacher could be eaten alive. The point is that each of us has to do what we feel comfortable with within the boundaries of the teacher-student relationship in order to establish trusting relationships with others.

IMPROVING YOUR RELATIONSHIP BUILDING CAPACITIES

Although trust is a central ingredient of helping relationships, it is not enough. Teachers who are effective helpers have developed a repertoire of qualities and skills that support their efforts to sustain helping relationships. They evaluate their communication skills to improve their classroom interactions; they conduct frequent checks of reality to assess the quality of their helping relationships.

Although they are willing to go the extra mile for their students, these teachers work at keeping informed about resources and referrals in their communities where they can send their students and families for help when their needs exceed what teachers can provide. School psychologists, school counselors, and administrators are trained specialists in helping students. When faced with serious problems for which they feel their skills are underdeveloped, areas in which they feel uncomfortable talking, such as lifestyle choices or pregnancy, or just too many demands on their time, classroom teachers will make a referral to another trained professional.

When making referrals with students, effective teachers need to explain that although they are pleased or flattered that students come to them with a problem, they are not the best people to offer the help or guidance in a given situation or are not comfortable with the issue, and they need to refer them to a professional. They carefully watch for the students' responses so as not to "put off" the students. They offer support by providing contact information and explaining the counseling process (perhaps even pointing out how that process has already begun with the initial conversations the teachers had with the students). They also follow up with students from time to time to see how things are going, showing their concern.

When a distraught teenage student confided in me (E. K.) that she was doing a lot of drinking because she felt pressure from her family to join in with them as they sat around the television every weekend and drank beer, I was pleased that she trusted me enough to confide in me. I was also quick to learn that my helping expertise was limited, and that I needed to find those sources of assistance in the community where my students and their families could receive confidential, effective support. As a result of the relationship I had fostered with this girl, I was able to convince her to speak to her counselor for additional help.

Let us assume that you agree that the teaching relationship is indeed the basis for learning in the classroom or in any other setting. How, then, do you develop the skills, qualities, knowledge, or whatever it takes to create these alliances? Developing effective teaching relationships depends primarily on two factors: (a) the attitudes that you communicate to others, and (b) your proficiency in communication skills (for other factors see Karns, 1994). You will find the following principles and skills discussed in this and the next chapter useful to you, not only in your classroom demeanor, but especially during those times when you are interacting with students in more informal settings, when they approach you for help on some matter or when you are the one to initiate the conversation.

Some Helpful Attitudes

Think about your times of greatest need, when you were really having problems and needed help. You struggled with a thorny issue, one with some difficult challenges. In deciding whom you would approach for assistance, whether it would be a close friend or relative, a coach or teacher, or a counselor, you reviewed in your mind whom *you* could trust the most. This means choosing not just people you could trust to keep things confidential and private, but also people who would not judge or criticize you or attempt to impose their beliefs on you. You preferred someone who could listen to you, who would really hear you and then help you to find your own way through the difficulty. This is exactly the sort of attitude that everyone else would want in a helper as well, whether in a counselor's office or a classroom.

Before you ever open your mouth, there are myriad internal tasks that must be completed to create a helping relationship. These include things related to the state of mind you adopt, one that is distinctly different from that of other relationships. Once you have decided to be helpful to another, a whole set of rules begins to operate that is otherwise dormant.

First, you must clear your mind of all distractions and focus your concentration on the person(s) you are helping. Give the student your complete and undivided attention, communicating with your eyes, your facial expressions, your posture and body position, every part of your being that you are intensely interested in what this person has to say. Beginning helpers often discover, much to their surprise, that this simple act of deliberate attending to another person is often enough to help the person to open up. It is so rare, after all, that we ever have anyone else's undivided attention.

Picture a typical classroom scene in which a student cautiously approaches a teacher at her desk. The teacher is obviously busy grading assignments and entering notations in her grade book. She is hurrying to complete the task so she can use her usual preparation period to catch up on some other work she has to do. Yet, here stands this child waiting for some attention.

"Yes, Maggie," the teacher says with impatience, "what can I do for you?"

"Well, um, I guess it's not that important. It can wait until another time."

The teacher looks up from her papers, placing her finger on a spot in the grade book so she doesn't lose her place. "No, that's okay, what do you want?" As the child starts to speak, the teacher's eyes flick down toward her unfinished work.

"It's just that there's been some stuff going on, and I'm not sure what to do about it."

"Go on," the teacher prompts. She is saying all the right things, encouraging the student to speak what is on her mind, but her nonverbal behavior and attitudes are communicating something other than complete interest.

Notice in all the conversations you have during a typical day how often people (and you) are doing other things—looking around, waving to others, rearranging clothes—at the same time that they (you) are talking. Similarly, notice how wonderful it feels to speak to someone who is doing everything in her power to communicate that she is hanging on your every word. She is using her eyes and her smile, her head nods, and she offers verbal acknowledgments to show that she is indeed following you closely.

Nonverbal attending behaviors like these are an important part of communicating helpful attitudes to others. Research has demonstrated that more than half of a communicated message is delivered by nonverbal channels (Leathers, 1996). This means that what you do is at least as important as what you say.

For children to open up and trust you, they must feel that you accept them as people, that you are nonjudgmental and noncritical of them as human beings. This does not at all mean that you accept everything that *they* might say or do; on the contrary, there may be many things *about their behavior* that you find unacceptable or inappropriate. The point is that you are able to separate your disapproval of what children are doing from who they are as persons.

This nonjudgmental attitude is even manifest in the way you speak to children. Instead of implying that you dislike them because of what they are doing, you may wish to word admonishments *very* carefully and sensitively: "Carlos, I don't like what you're doing right now, and I need for you to stop." It is crucial for Carlos to feel that although you will not tolerate his acting out in class, you still genuinely care for him and accept him as a person.

This may very well be one of the most difficult aspects of helping in general—and of teaching in particular—for acceptance of others requires a great deal of tolerance, sensitivity, and cultural awareness. It means that you are knowledgeable about the diverse backgrounds from which your children originate, and that you demonstrate respect for their individual and cultural differences. When you can model this in your own behavior, then you can teach children to be tolerant of one another's differences.

Improving Your Relationship Skills

You are clear. You feel neutral and open. You have focused your concentration on the task at hand. You are attending fully to your learner(s). You take a deep breath, and you begin. If only it was this simple! In fact, when using relationship skills, there are no fewer than 60 different behaviors involved (Nelson-Jones, 1990). Most of these can be divided into several broad categories, each of which follows logically from its predecessor.

For your purposes, we present a summary of some basic things to keep in mind when building relationships with students (see Table 3.1). In the chapters that follow, we describe these skills more thoroughly. You will also wish to consult other sources that can help you to improve your helping proficiency.

The first set of skills, naturally, would involve *assessing the student's needs*. The best relationships—learning, helping, or personal—are those in which the other people feel that their needs are being met. Although we mentioned earlier that children often do not identify a need for school-based education, they do feel a strong motive to learn and grow, especially under the wing of a wise and respected mentor. Assessing children's needs requires that you listen attentively, ask pertinent questions, and help them to articulate what they want.

Stop for a moment and consider what kids would say if they were asked what they desire most in their lives. Better yet, go out and talk to children about the same age as those you would like to teach. Interview them systematically about their greatest desires and most important priorities. We think you will find that most children would probably say that they want to be entertained, to be loved and appreciated; they want to have fun, to play, to laugh, to have a good time. They want good friends. They want their parents to get along. They want nice things. They would also say they do not mind working if it is toward some goal that seems worthwhile.

Table 3.1   A Checklist of Things to Remember When Talking to Students

---

Your attitudes
- Stay clear
- Be nonjudgmental
- Feel accepting
- Be authentic
- Feel compassionate

Your nonverbal behaviors
- Pay attention
- Maintain eye contact
- Communicate interest with face and body
- Express warmth

Your strategies
- Be supportive
- Show empathy
- Prove you have heard and understood
- Keep your focus on the student

Exploration skills come next in the unfolding process of building a helping relationship. Children are encouraged to freely examine their thoughts and feelings regarding what they are experiencing. They are encouraged to share these perceptions aloud. Our job is to help them to become more aware of what is going on inside themselves, as well as what is going on around them. We use our helping skills to facilitate their exploration of the internal and external world.

What this looks like in a classroom situation involves a teacher paying attention not only to the *content* of what is being communicated but also to the underlying *process* of the message. In the following example of promoting exploration of feelings as well as thoughts, a teacher helps her class to explore their deeper reactions to a discussion on conflict related to characters in a story they were reading.

Teacher: So, what many of you seem to be saying is that you think it's wrong for people to argue for their ideas if it means hurting someone else.

Megan: Not exactly. I mean, in the story we read, the person just had to say something. And she wasn't being listened to, so she had to do something to get their attention. She didn't mean to hurt anyone.

Teacher: What about you, Megan? What about a time in your life when someone's feelings got hurt as a result of something you said? You didn't mean to be hurtful. You just tried to get your point across.

Megan: Yeah. That happens a lot with my sister.

Teacher: What about some others of you who can think of times in which this has happened?

Michael: I remember one time when you hurt my feelings by cutting me off.

The class breaks out in laughter. Michael tucks his head under his arm in embarrassment.

Teacher: I agree with you, Michael. That's a good example of exactly what we're talking about. I was so much in a hurry to get through the lesson that I forgot to pay attention to how some of you were reacting to things I was saying and doing. So, in the story, how do they resolve their disagreement? And what can we learn from that to apply in our own lives?

In this scenario, the teacher is probing the students to make connections between events that took place in a story and those in their own lives. She is helping them to relate the themes to their lived experiences. And she is doing so using mostly exploratory relationship skills, asking a few open-ended questions and expanding the discussion to include process as well as content elements. This exploration quite naturally leads to some deeper levels of understanding.

In the third stage of helping, some degree of *insight* or *understanding* is fostered. We challenge children to look critically, objectively, and sometimes emotionally at what they are learning. We present new ideas; help them to articulate their concerns and confusion, and then facilitate the integration of these perceptions into their own thinking. This involves not only introducing them to concepts but also helping them to personalize the relevance of the material to their own lives in much the same way that we just illustrated. True understanding is not just something that we know intellectually; rather it is something that we have made part of us, resulting in changes in the way we behave, reason, and feel about ourselves and others.

The transition from understanding to action cannot take place unless children are willing to get outside of their comfort zones. Teachers who are skilled at developing good relationships are able to encourage children to translate what they know into something *they can do*. Tanya, for example, is extremely shy. She is very well behaved, a teacher's dream, if that teacher likes obedient, passive children who sit quietly and rarely say anything. The theme in today's history class is "order and disorder in the universe." The kids have a lot to say about the subject; they understand only too well about the way chaos rules their lives—everyone but Tanya, that is, who usually sits serene and Buddha-like at her desk. She is writing furiously in her notebook. Something has hit home for her.

The teacher notices Tanya's uncharacteristic animation and invites her to share her perceptions aloud. She politely declines by averting her eyes and shaking her head. The lesson moves along. After class, Tanya slinks by the teacher's desk, but not before he asks to speak with her for a few minutes during his next prep period. In this one-on-one situation, she feels a lot more comfortable expressing herself and proceeds to do just that—unleashing a barrage of pent-up feelings about how helpless and frustrated she feels. Related to the theme in class, her home life is a model of disorder and chaos. She never knows what to expect when she gets home, who will be spending the night, or what kind of mood her family will be in.

The teacher gently prods Tanya to talk about the things she had written down during class, ideas that are quite perceptive. Her conclusion is that order can never be created from disorder without decisive action to disrupt the usual patterns. The teacher readily agrees and then asks her how that principle applies to her own life. At first she is puzzled, then her face lights up and then darkens again, and she shrugs in frustration: How can she ever change things that are out of her control?

There are some things that are definitely within her control, however, most notably how she chooses to respond to the chaos around her, even in the very class that she is in. Tanya has developed a clear awareness of the problems, but that is not enough; she must find a way to incorporate this insight into her behavior so that she can function more effectively in her life. The place to start, the teacher gently suggests, is in class. "What would it take for you to overcome the chaos you feel inside and venture outside yourself far enough to reveal what you think and feel?"

As Tanya is helped to convert her understanding into action, so must all learning become incorporated in behavior. Teachers who have highly developed relationship skills are able to facilitate this process through the trust that they are able to create, a safety that invites children to experiment and to take constructive risks. In Tanya's case, it was her teacher's willingness to offer support that gave her the strength she needed to find her voice and break out of her shell.

Relationships in a Teacher's Life

The true beauty of these relationship skills is that they are applied with equal effectiveness to all human connections, including those with your colleagues, friends, and family members. Once you make yourself into a relationship specialist, supremely skilled at developing trust and safety with those whom you help, there is no reason you cannot do so in other areas of your life.

It never ceases to amaze us how hypocritical some members of our profession can be. As teachers, we supposedly are models of wisdom and learning. Apart from any content we pass along, the human dimension of our job is to impart values of truth seeking, honesty, integrity, and compassion. Yet, so often we see teachers who appear so "together" in their classes and so spectacularly ineffective in their lives. Or, they cannot practice in their own lives what they say is so important for their students to do or to be. They preach in their classes about how valuable it is to study hard, but they no longer work with the degree of commitment that they expect from others. They demand that their students stretch themselves, yet they are doing essentially the same things they have been doing for a long time. They ask their students to be good citizens, to be kind and respectful toward one another, yet they are somewhat less than caring in the ways that they relate to others in their school. Not only do these discrepancies compromise their professional effectiveness because students are incredibly aware of hypocrisy, but teachers also surrender such a wonderful benefit of the job: the opportunity to apply relationship skills where they matter the most—with those you love.

If you have trained yourself to become an attentive and compassionate listener, just imagine how easily those habits can be translated into the natural ways you relate to everyone in your life. If you develop the ability to read students' nonverbal cues and innermost feelings, this interpersonal sensitivity becomes just as useful with loved ones. When you learn to present yourself in class as confident, knowledgeable, and influential, there is no reason why you cannot become more persuasive at home and with friends. The more skill and sensitivity with which you do your work at school, the more able you are to become a better friend, parent, partner, and colleague.

Suggested Activities

1. With a partner, practice the skills mentioned in this chapter. Take turns talking about an issue while giving the speaker undivided attention. Pay attention to the body language as well as the spoken words. Reflect what you have heard to show you were paying attention.

2. Observe teachers in the classroom and note how many nonverbal interactions they have with students through eye contact, gestures, smiles, maybe even a wink of encouragement.

3. Discuss with others how teachers build relationships with students and how they show they care for their students—through their words, actions, and the environment they create.

CHAPTER FOUR

On Being an Effective Communicator

> *Identify a pool of highly successful teachers, and you will be surprised to discover how very different they are as persons and as professionals. These teaching superstars utilize different strategies and express different ideas about maintaining student discipline. Contrast their classrooms, and you find major differences in how they structure learning environments for their students. Some utilize student learning centers; others cluster students in cooperative learning groups. Some teachers individualize their classroom space with separate study carrels; others arrange their rooms traditionally with students sitting in straight rows. As different as these highly successful teachers may be, there is one critical feature they share: They are all accomplished communicators.*

PRINCIPLES OF EFFECTIVE CLASSROOM COMMUNICATION

Our classrooms are populated by people whose success largely depends on verbal and nonverbal communication. The skills presented in this chapter are intended to help you establish a base you can use to plan and evaluate all those elements that go together to support effective teacher-student, student-teacher, and student-student modes of communication. Without an intentional communication base, it is likely that a teacher will revert to the "boss-manager" approach that Glasser (1998) and others find so coercive.

There are five basic principles that we would like you to keep in mind as you develop your repertoire of effective communication skills. Although hardly an exhaustive list, these points should act as reminders of the most important things to consider in the classroom or, for that matter, in any relationship in your life.

Principle 1: Provide a Base of Genuine Caring

The foundation for effective classroom communication must rest on a genuine caring for all students. Noddings (1984), a philosopher of education, is adamant in her assertion that there is a crisis of caring in our schools that manifests in students feeling that nobody values them, and consequently, they do not know how to be care-givers to others.

Some teachers mistakenly substitute "taking care of" for "having care for" their students. Edward is one of these sincere but misguided teachers. If you visited his sophomore English composition class, you would often hear him soothe the anxiety of certain students with words such as, "Don't worry about your writing, Cecily, I'll take care of you!" Consequently, students such as Cecily stop worrying about their writing; in fact, they stop writing altogether. They enter into a tacit agreement with Edward: He will not make any demands of them to communicate in writing, and they will not use their idle time in his class to be disruptive.

Teachers display genuine caring for students when they find out about students' abilities and motivations. They continue this perva-sive caring by providing all their students with the appropriate amount of support, structure, and expectations they need to be self-directed, responsible learners. Anne is one of these genuinely caring teachers. Her fifth graders demonstrate reading and math skills from first- to tenth-grade levels. "I don't let any of them off the hook; I don't give up on any of them," she maintains. She communicates with a tone of obvious concern about their performance. Students' hard work in her class is not motivated by fear of their teacher or because of other negative consequences. It comes from within, built on a sustained sense of pride and enthusiasm for their personal, real accomplishments as learners.

There is one last dimension to caring that provides a solid base for a powerful climate of effective classroom communication. The caring must not only extend from teacher to student and student to teacher, but it must also be demonstrated in the caring students show for each other. Without the mutual esteem of students for one another, the classroom climate will not be conducive to trust and openness. When students are not taught and encouraged to care about and to cooperate with one another, we can expect to see a highly competitive climate where some students are assigned high academic status, some average status, and the remainder low academic status. The results? It is difficult to feel motivated to work in an environment in which you have been marginalized or labeled as incompetent.

In creating a positive social environment Olweus (2003) writes of four important principles from his research on preventing bullying. These can also be applied to the classroom setting in general. The most critical variables include: (1) warmth and interest from the teacher, (2) enforceable limits of unacceptable behavior, (3) consistent follow-through when rules are broken, and (4) acting as positive role models. Teachers must implement routines for safety, procedures for efficient use of time, and rules for behavior to support learning for all students. Disrespect, bullying, and other forms of harassment are not to be tolerated. By supervising and monitoring student behavior, teachers convey high expectations and regard for all.

Principle 2: All Students Can Be Effective Communicators

The second principle of effective classroom communications is a logical extension of our discussion about the "caring base." Teachers who genuinely care about all their children will not give up on any of them. Peggy and Diane team teach a first-grade class. Two of their students, Jesse and Joe, struggle with the demands of their learning tasks and frequently act out their frustrations with all kinds of disruptive behaviors, from getting out of their seats whenever the spirit moves them to making fart noises and other disruptive sounds. These two caring teachers, however, maintain a quiet resolve that these students will learn to be responsive and responsible classroom communicators. They have assigned Jesse and Joe to seats in the front of the class, where they can more easily communicate with these active boys and keep them on task. They measure their success by the small yet steady progress made by these two challenging students. In addition to receiving the caring of their teachers, those students who struggle with a variety of learning problems and disabilities can be enabled to become effective learners by caring peers working together in cooperative learning groups.

Cooperative learning activities provide students with the opportunity to use their multiple abilities to solve problems and complete significant tasks (Cohen & Goodlad, 1994; Johnson & Johnson, 1999). One of my (E. K.) favorite activities is called, "Think, Pair, Share." After posing a question, I ask students to first formulate a personal response; then, turn to a partner; and finally, share their responses with each other. If time permits, I'll ask students to share their conversations with the whole class.

Beginning teachers will want to have students work with partners with specific directions for a concrete task for short periods, gradually extending the allotted time. For example, pieces or clues to a mystery can be distributed to each group where only by working together will students be successful. It is helpful for students to practice being attentive to and cooperating with a partner in performing an activity before working in a small group.

Cooperative learning exercises involve teams or small groups working together to help each other learn (Slavin, 1988). Teachers assign students to mixed ability groups, with four students to a group taking into consideration academic ability, language proficiency, gender, and ethnicity. Students solve problems, study for a test making sure each person has mastered the lesson or unit objectives, or jigsaw information—where representatives from each group become experts in an area and share with the entire group. Although students work together and receive recognition for their team accomplishments, there is also individual assessment for accountability.

We also suggest having students practice the attitudes and skills mentioned in the previous chapter—being nonjudgmental, maintaining eye contact, being supportive. Assign a role or roles to each member of the group to keep them involved and rotate responsibilities. These roles might be timekeeper, recorder, reporter, encourager/monitor, group process observer, with other duties related to the task, such as artist or materials and supplies facilitator. As students gain experience working with various classmates, they will be able to work effectively in small groups with more complex tasks. It is important to debrief the cooperative experience with students as well as assess what was learned. Have group members explore to what extent they were able to work together successfully and were able to reach the goals set for the groups.

The ultimate classroom communication goal will be to establish a genuine community of students, teachers, parents, and other outside resource people, who use all sorts of real communications, in the form of talk, debate, drama, mime, role playing, storytelling, demonstrations, letters, newsletters, puppets, artwork, short stories, poems, and any other form of human discourse used to communicate heartfelt thoughts and feelings.

Principle 3: Planning for Effective Classroom Communication

Effective communications between teachers and students will not just happen in classrooms on a regular basis. If left unplanned, classroom communications remain accidental and incidental at best. This also gives students the message that meaningful talk, responsive listening, and authentic writing, at least by students, are not very important in school. This message is not a far cry from "children should be seen, but not heard."

Carolyn, a junior high social studies teacher, makes some form of student response a part of each of her classes. Watch her in action, and you will see the careful planning she uses to encourage students to speak confidently about past and present social issues. In her daily planning, this culturally sensitive teacher prepares experiences that provide opportunities for students from culturally diverse backgrounds to share their views, experiences, and beliefs with the entire class (Banks, 1993).

Carolyn has found that this consistent practice provides most of her students with positive benefits. It helps build the confidence of her minority students to participate in all forms of classroom communication—large group, small group, and individual conferences—with genuine confidence. It also helps minority students to clarify and affirm their cultural values. Majority culture students benefit in two major ways. First, they come to know and appreciate their culturally diverse peers, their values and beliefs. Second, they come to recognize that their minority peers can be effective communicators. This benefit has enabled Carolyn and her students to establish a classroom climate largely free of the academic status disorders that prevent many minority students from having access to the channels of successful classroom communications (see Cohen, 1994; Hernandez, 2000; Rosenholtz, 1985).

Carolyn also prepares her students for active and responsible listening. She rearranges student desks into small groups for problem-solving activities. She often uses a fishbowl structure, with students sitting in three concentric circles for debates and discussions.

Students in the inner circle share their arguments or ideas, and the student seated just behind serve as resource people, providing additional details or important information. The students in the outside circle are listening intently and making notes in preparation for their turn in the inner circle 10 minutes later. This type of teacher preparation of the structure and learning experiences ensures active student involvement in effective classroom communications. It makes all students responsible for active listening, critical thinking, and responsible speaking. It also keeps them on their toes because class structures remain dynamic rather than stale.

Morning Meeting and Democratic Classrooms

Teachers at the primary grade level know the importance of careful planning for making classroom communications more effective. Kriete (2003) describes morning meetings developed as a part of the Responsive Classroom approach of the Northeast Foundation for Children. Students (and their teacher) begin their day in a circle to greet one another, and each day, selected students share something significant about their preferences or interests. After each presentation, responses are invited (always respectful and supportive in tone), followed by a group activity and a discussion of current events. The chart below identifies each component and its benefit.

Through morning meetings teachers create a sense of community while guiding students in the development of their communication skills and in building relationships with one another. Together they create a warm environment in which each student will feel secure and be heard, building trust and respect in a place where students will feel comfortable not only working together but taking risks.

Teachers at the secondary level, as well as at the elementary level, establish democratic classrooms to involve students in taking responsibility for their learning. They allow students to participate in establishing classroom rules, arranging the physical environment,

Morning Meeting

Activity	Skills
Greeting	Students learn each other's names; receive recognition from peers while practicing verbal skills that build relationships.
Sharing	Speakers learn to take turns, speak in front of peers, while listeners learn something about each other and how to appropriately respond and/or ask questions related to personal comments.
Group activity (song, chant, game, poem)	Whether a fun activity or an academic skill builder, students learn to follow directions in order to do something together, developing language skills and building familiarity, a sense of belonging to a community, and a sense of history.
News and announcements	While developing reading skills (teacher reading, echo reading, choral reading), students receive a welcome message as a group and each student receives the information about the day's activities at the same time, creating a sense of group identity.

and where possible, determining options in their learning activities. Although it takes time at the beginning of the school year to engage students in the process of coming to consensus or voting on decisions as to how the class will operate, it is well worth the effort. Students feel respected and valued for their input and have more "buy-in" with respect to the decisions. In fact, Parkay and Stanford (2001) found that research shows teachers who involve their students in decisions that relate to their classes experience fewer behavior problems.

"For most teachers, their relationships *are* their teaching. The underlying principles of a democratic classroom—choice, discourse, social responsibility, community, critical inquiry, authentic learning, and teaching a relevant and creative curriculum—help promote caring relationships between teachers and students" (Wolk, 2003, p. 14). Wolk offers the following four ways to build a classroom community in which the development of relationships and meaningful learning occur:

Building Classroom Community

Activity	Benefit
Discussion and debate of important and controversial issues	Students learn their opinions matter and are trusted to discuss important ideas.
Murals and collages	Students take pride in their work; ownership in the classroom environment while focusing on themes raises the level of thinking in the work.
Drama and role playing	Students work together on a common task and have an opportunity to move around while reinforcing what they have learned and making connections.
Games	Students learn communication skills and positive relationships.

As a final note, you should not be surprised that Wolk favors culturally relevant, inquiry-based curriculum, discussed in previous chapters, connecting all learning to the student's world.

Principle 4: Make Classroom Communications Realistic

Among the most popular television shows that have ever appeared, from *Candid Camera* and *Real People* to *America's Funniest Home Videos, Survivor,* and *The Apprentice,* are those that portray human beings in their most natural state. There is something absolutely captivating about seeing people operate spontaneously. There also is tremendous relief in the shared experiences of realizing that we are not alone in the silly, unpredictable, and yet authentically human things we do when we are alone.

In one research study (Kottler, 1990), consisting of 1,500 interviews with people describing what they do in their most private moments, the same themes return again and again. When we are alone, we are able to be more natural, more spontaneous and uninhibited, more able to give vent to our creative spirits. The public image we present to the world is temporarily suspended when we are in our own company. In solitude, we are free to talk to ourselves, dance and sing, make funny faces in the mirror, wear what we like, and do what we want whenever we feel like it. Of course, if someone else spies on us engaging in these solitary activities, it makes for hilarious entertainment.

Teachers need to help students to be real people in classroom learning experiences, as well as in their private lives. Barry is an award-winning high school English teacher. Drop in on his class from time to time, and you will see these real people in action. Barry's students do not study textbooks to memorize the format for a business letter they may need to write during their adult lives some five years in the future. They use their textbooks as resources to help them select the proper format for a letter that they write and send now— about issues that are important to them now. One of his students wrote a letter to a newspaper editor critical of the treatment of senior citizens in a retirement home. The letter was about real people—the real concerns of the student communicator. It also prompted a heated rejoinder from the proprietor, who presented some evidence about which the student writer was not aware. The interchange made the student writer more careful to document his claims; it also resulted in better care for residents in the nursing home.

Realistic forms of communication, such as those used in Barry's classroom, encourage active student engagement, as well as spontaneous, authentic encounters. They also promote oral and written language that is animated by the fresh and vibrant voices of the student communicators. Given opportunities to participate actively in experiences of significance to their lives as people right now, students will respond in an enthusiastic, caring, and responsible form of communication with teachers and with each other.

Principle 5: Regular Practice for Effective Communications

The last principle of effective classroom communication is so simple and obvious that you may consider it unnecessary. If students in our elementary and secondary schools received regular opportunities for real experiences in classroom communication, this principle would be unnecessary. Unfortunately, in too many of our classrooms, students are busy studying about effective listening, speaking, and writing instead of being regularly engaged in meaningful communications. Many language arts classrooms, which should be havens of real student talking and writing, are often judged effective by principals if students are quietly copying sentences from a book or filling in the blanks for a grammar task.

Consider having your students engage in a real-life problem (at the school level for elementary students and in the community for secondary students), research the history, identify and or/develop solutions, and present them to the appropriate institution or agency. I (E. K.) recall a colleague whose students actively campaigned for a street light in front of their school after several car accidents occurred. These students had to prepare for a hearing in front of the city council and were successful in their effort. This was an experience those students will never forget, one in which they developed communication skills that will serve them the rest of their lives.

Look for possible inquiry learning, project-based learning, or service learning opportunities related to your subject area; often they can provide motivating and meaningful experiences that go beyond the classroom into the community. Have students write or speak to real audiences. Invite students at other grade levels, parents, guardians, and members of the community to act as an authentic audience.

As you continue to construct the image of the kind of teacher you want to be, reflect on these principles and resolve that you will provide your students with a variety of regular opportunities for real communication with you and their classmates, based on genuine caring for each other. If you are successful in becoming the image of the terrific teacher you have the power to be, your classroom will become a community of real people who care for one another, a community that supports all of the members' growth as competent and confident communicators.

THE SKILLS OF EFFECTIVE COMMUNICATION FOR PERSONAL ISSUES

During the 1970s, Thomas Gordon (1974) popularized the notion that parents and teachers could learn to be a lot more effective in their interactions with children if only they would devote time to mastering some basic communication skills. In a series of training programs he developed, Gordon presented the essential skills that he found most useful in resolving interpersonal conflicts, solving problems, and generally fostering better communication.

For the first step in deciding which communication strategy to employ, Gordon felt it was important to determine who actually "owns" the problem, the student or the teacher. So often, communication efforts fail because one or both parties fail to assess accurately what the other one really wants from the exchange.

Who's Got the Problem?

Applying the communication strategies for solving interpersonal conflicts can help teachers develop the skills and habits they need to maintain order in their classrooms while providing a safe classroom climate that encourages authentic communication. In the following scenarios, decide for yourself who has the problem, the student or the teacher?

Fred is carving his initials in the desk.
☐ Student has the problem.   ☐ Teacher has the problem.

Gwen and Natalie are whispering and passing notes to one another.
☐ Student has the problem.   ☐ Teacher has the problem.

Candy is asleep at her desk.
☐ Student has the problem.   ☐ Teacher has the problem.

Rick refuses to comply with directions.
☐ Student has the problem.   ☐ Teacher has the problem.

In each of these instances, if you guessed the students had the problem, and you tried to solve it with an intervention, Gordon would contend that *you* are missing the point. All of these cases illustrate behavior that is disturbing to the teacher, not to the student. Now, of course, the students may (and probably do) have underlying problems of their own. But these target behaviors are really the teacher's problems, because the teacher is the one who wants the behaviors to stop.

Normally, a teacher might respond to the boy carving up the desk as follows: "Young man! Do you have a problem with behaving yourself?" The student is, of course, thinking to himself, "Teacher, the only problem I have is you."

A teacher might say to noncompliant students, such as students who are whispering: "You are in big trouble if you don't stop that!"

In each example, however, these interventions that attempt to place the problem on the student are dishonest and inaccurate. In reality, because it is the teacher who is most bothered with the behavior, it is the teacher's problem. Any attempt to try to solve a problem that is based on erroneous assumptions is going to prove less effective than those that imply more direct and focused communication.

I Versus You

The "I-message" is the preferred form of communication in these circumstances, rather than those that point a finger with "you." I-messages are more honest portrayals of what is taking place. For several reasons, they are more useful in situations in which you own the problem:

- They are perceived as less challenging and threatening.
- They focus on behavior rather than on criticizing the person.
- They model effective ways of being assertive and of taking care of yourself.

Contrast the differences between "you" and "I" messages in the following two cases:

1. A student throws a paper wad at you.

    You-message: You are a bad boy! It's not nice for you to be so mean and inconsiderate.

    I-message: Oh. That surprised me. I feel hurt, and I don't like to be treated this way.

2. Two students will not stop talking in the back of the room.

    You-message: Do the two of you have a problem back there?

    I-message: I have a problem with the two of you talking while I am trying to present this material.

This is much more than a matter of mere semantics. I-messages are clear statements about what you think and feel regarding what is taking place. They let students know that you have a problem with certain behaviors that you consider to be unacceptable. In your interventions, you communicate your dissatisfaction without placing blame and without attacking, yet you firmly indicate that you want the behavior to stop. You honestly and clearly acknowledge that the problem is yours and that you need some help to resolve the problem.

In other circumstances, it may be the student, rather than you, who has the problem. (Of course, when students do not respond to I-messages, it is easy to make your problem theirs as well.) In these cases, such as when a child acknowledges having some difficulty, "active listening" is the preferred mode of communication.

Active Listening in Action

In the next chapter, we discuss at greater length how communication skills can be used to help children with their problems. Here we consider active listening as a style of relating to others that invites them to be open and honest about what they are thinking and feeling. In active listening, the teacher takes a direct role in responding to what a student says by paraphrasing what was said and acknowledging the feelings expressed. Listening is communicated by the way you respond to the speaker proving you heard what was said and how the person feels about it. Witness, for example, how active listening skills can be incorporated into normal classroom dialogue.

Teacher: Who can tell me about a famous Impressionist painter that you read about in your chapter, one who really seemed interesting to you?

David: Van Gogh!

Teacher: That's great. David, why do you like Van Gogh so much?

David: 'Cause he was so unusual. He was different. Not like other people. His paintings were so expressive, so much a part of him. He even got so carried away with emotions that one time he cut off his ear.

The class laughs, although David's expression remains quite serious. His lip quivers.

Teacher: David, you wonder if the class is laughing at you?

David: No, I just don't think it's so funny.

Teacher: It really bothers you that people would laugh at others who are different and who live with so much pain?

David does not answer. He nods his head and then averts his eyes.

Teacher: And the parts of Van Gogh that you can easily relate to—the part about not feeling understood sometimes?

David: (Softly) Yes, I guess so. It's just that it really bothers me that someone who was so talented and so creative was just ignored most of his life.

Teacher: Thank you, David, for your very perceptive observations. Who else would like to comment on what they felt was interesting?

As can be seen from this dialogue, the teacher is able to accomplish several important tasks as a result of using active listening communication skills. Note that the teacher accomplishes all of the following process goals in addition to the content goals of the lesson:

- She builds trust among and with her students, who feel that it is safe for them to be open and to share their feelings.
- She demonstrates respect for them as intelligent truth seekers and thereby encourages self-respect.
- She is careful to reinforce and support sharing—so others feel safe to talk and explore their ideas.
- She promotes acceptance of individual differences and encourages students to accept one another.
- Through her responses, she communicates that she has heard and understood what students are saying.
- She moves students to deeper levels of understanding about the subject (Van Gogh) and about themselves.
- She models a way of being with people that is warm and supportive.
- She encourages the free exchange of ideas.

Because this sensitive teacher is adept not only at addressing and assessing the effectiveness of her art appreciation lesson but also in listening to and responding to the authentic feelings and ideas of her students, she is able to create an environment for honest communication in which students can feel safe to explore ideas, affirm their own values, and take risks without fear of put-downs. Armed with this dual vision for meeting both the instructional goals and the learning needs of her students, this teacher will not need to manage student behaviors with coercion.

Supplementing class discussion or as an alternate activity, many teachers engage in dialogue journals with their students where students complete entries either to a given prompt or on a self-initiated basis, and teachers respond by passing the journal back and forth. Some students will take advantage of the written format and go into greater depth with their teachers. Journaling is an excellent way to keep communication going on an individual basis with students especially when class sizes are large.

COMMUNICATION WITH PARENTS AND GUARDIANS

Communicating with parents and guardians is an ongoing activity. Through newsletters, progress reports, notes sent home, Web sites, and e-mail, teachers communicate in writing. With digital cameras, it is easier than ever to send or post pictures for parents to see. We are continuously providing information, setting goals, and reviewing progress with parents and guardians regarding academic, behavioral, and social development of their children. We regularly send home examples of student work. Whether in a room full of adults at Open House or Back to School Night, in a parent conference, or on the telephone, good oral communication skills are vital. We must also make them feel comfortable and communicate our interest, thereby providing a base of caring. We must plan what we are going to say, how we will approach the topic, and have examples of student work and/or behavior and grades available as a reference. Active listening will be very important, first, in hearing what the parents have to say—as they will often provide insight into the child's behavior—and second, in working with them to develop action plans to support their child during the school year.

Parent Conferences

Some of the most challenging—and important—aspects of a teacher's job involve communications with parents and guardians of students. After all, without their cooperation and support, much of our efforts are wasted.

Successful parent conferences need careful planning before they begin. Factors to consider include the following:

1. The reason for the conference. Who initiated the meeting, and what is the agenda? If the parents initiated the meeting, it is likely you will do a lot of listening, letting the parents or guardians know that you have heard and understood the stated concerns. If you are the one who initiated the meeting, then you are likely to do more questioning and information gathering.

2. Convenient setting. It is important that the meetings be arranged at a mutually convenient time with no interruptions.

3. Support materials. You will want to have on hand any papers, test results, examples of student work, records, or grades, as well as descriptions of behavior that might support points that are raised.

4. Translator. You will need help if the parents or guardians do not speak English fluently (or you do not speak their language).

5. Agenda. Make sure you have clearly stated expectations for student progress, strengths and weaknesses, and an action plan for the future. Often this is negotiated in the meeting.

6. Participants. Decide whether the student should be included in the meeting. At times this may be awkward or inappropriate, but in some circumstances it helps the student to feel part of the team, rather than an object who is labeled as a problem. Some conference strategies even empower the student to lead the meeting and accept responsibility for planning the conference, as well as the outcomes.

7. Creating comfort. Help the participants to feel at ease as much as possible, given the potentially stressful circumstances. Start on an upbeat note by saying something good about the child, or telling a short story that puts the student in

a positive frame. You can then elicit information about the student from the parents by asking open-ended questions about the child and what the child has said about the class.

Guillaume (2004) reminds us to appreciate rather than to evaluate families' successes and struggles with their children. Her other tips include paraphrasing what parents say to show you understand, keeping things positive, and using humor to keep things in perspective. Remember to reflect the content and the feelings expressed by the parents.

8. Share your observations. Explain the expectations and agenda for the meeting. Provide the parents with information from your records. Review student work. Avoid the educational jargon that so easily becomes a part of a teacher's vocabulary. Address any issues that arise, eliciting help from parents as you identify specific strategies they can use to support their children. Determine with the parents what, if anything, can be done, as well as when and how this might be accomplished. Finally, decide how progress will be monitored.

9. End the conference on a positive note. Extend compliments where appropriate. Invite each person to summarize the discussion. Thank the parents for coming and participating in the conference. Make a plan to continue communication.

Before a parent conference, I (E. K.) put together a folder with examples of student work and print a copy of the assignments, student attendance, and student grades. Then I clear away any clutter in the conference area and arrange comfortable seats for the parents so we can look at student work together. I greet the parents by name as they come in and give them a chance to look around the room. I begin by asking the parents what the child has said about the class to see what the parents know and to give the parents a chance to begin the conference and raise any concerns they might have. I do a lot of listening in the beginning and then guide the conversation to the expectations for the class and how the student is progressing. At the end, I summarize the main points of our dialogue. After the conference I take a few minutes to jot down notes regarding the discussion, reflect on how the conference proceeded, and note any follow-up activities that have been planned.

By asking open-ended questions we can learn much about the children from their parents as we learn about their backgrounds and cultures. Some children receive great support at home; while others do not. For some, crowded, noisy homes are problematic. Children from other countries may have experienced different types of schools so that they and their parents may be unfamiliar with our education system, teaching practices, and grading scales. Their parents may or may not actively support their education depending on their culture, even their learning and speaking of English, not to mention new cultural ways of dressing, eating, and socializing. Or, they may defer all decisions regarding education to you, the teacher, in whom they have the utmost respect and give deference to in such matters although, at first, it may seem as though they do not care.

There are many ways to get to know parents. Go to the school events, from concerts to athletic contests, where they will be present. Attend community events, such as fairs and parades. Invite parents into your classroom to talk about their occupations, other skills, or cultural backgrounds. Involve them as part of an audience for a play or debate, visitors to a museum or fair, jury for a mock trial. Ask them to help supervise an activity or field trip. Although some parents may be available regularly to help, others may greatly appreciate a one-day only request. Have a sign-up sheet at Open House where parents can indicate ways they can support your activities.

THE HUMAN DIMENSION OF CLASSROOM COMMUNICATIONS

We wish to mention one further point as you attempt to apply the principles and skills of communication included in this chapter. Although we treat this subject in a fairly technical manner, emphasizing the principles of establishing and maintaining classroom communications and describing the *skills* involved in relating to others, communication is a humanly lived activity. The human dimensions of communication include many intangibles that cannot be easily described or even identified.

To be an effective classroom communicator, one that invites every one of your students to be an active participant in a genuine open learning community, you will need to incorporate these concepts in your own interaction style. You will need to reflect on ways you can improve your classroom communications and enhance the unique ways you relate to others. Your style of self-expression is the primary means by which you will attempt to convey your thoughts, feelings, and ideas and to communicate your deep understanding of others' experiences.

SUGGESTED ACTIVITIES

1. Observe a small group of students working together. Identify their strengths and weaknesses as communicators.

2. In your relationships with your family, friends, and classmates, practice using I-messages.

3. Research authentic assessment projects for your subject area, ways to involve students in meaningful learning activities that will build their communication skills.

4. Observe a master teacher in a class discussion to see how process goals as well as content goals are reached.

5. Practice active listening with a partner. Ask your partner to talk about something that is personally meaningful. Then respond to what you heard (the content) and how the person felt about it (emotion or sentiment). Use statements, such as "You feel . . ." to see if you were able to appropriately identify the feeling. If not, have your partner correct you.

6. With a partner, role play a conference with a parent whose child is misbehaving during a class to practice active listening skills and giving I-messages.

7. Research trust building activities and collaborative, cooperative learning activities for the grade level and subject area in which you are interested.

CHAPTER FIVE

On Being a Helper

> *Close your eyes for a moment. Take a deep breath. Consider the child sitting opposite you. Meet this child's eyes. Concentrate. Concentrate with all your being on this child. Use all your energy and power to focus completely on this person. Resist all other distractions, both internal and external. Attend to this child fully, using your body, gestures, eyes, smile. Communicate with every part of you that you care deeply about this child, about what this child is saying. Assure the child of your undivided attention, your acceptance, your caring.*

These instructions form the barest glimmer of what is involved in a helping relationship. It is so rare that any of us feels truly heard and understood by another person. In so many of our relationships, with family, friends, the people we are closest to, we sort of half listen as we do other things simultaneously—glance at the paper, watch television, listen to the radio, stare out the window, wave to someone else passing by. We are all so hungry for someone to really listen to us, children most of all.

ATTRIBUTES OF HELPING RELATIONSHIPS

Helping relationships, those between teachers, counselors, or therapists and their clients, are about the only relationships in which children feel that they have someone else's full and complete attention. They are used to being treated as if what they have to say is not important. They are only kids, best seen but not heard. Even though teachers justifiably complain that they have neither the time nor the training to listen to children's problems, you can make a tremendous difference in students' lives by spending only a few minutes each day listening and responding to them. To do so, you must first understand how helping relationships are different from other intimate encounters.

Postponing Your Own Agenda

The commitment to be helpful to children means putting your own needs and issues aside. It means doing anything and everything in your power to help children reach their goals (as long as they are constructive). It means separating what is good for you versus what is good for the child, because sometimes these needs do not coincide. A teenager, for example, may be struggling with the decision to have an abortion and may have decided to follow through on this choice, even though you strongly object to abortion on moral grounds. With a friend or family member, it is perfectly fine to express your opinions in the most passionate terms, but in a helping relationship, you work within the student's value system, not your own. What you would do with your life is not often relevant to what your students should do with theirs.

This quality of helping relationships is so difficult to develop that counselors and therapists undergo years of training and supervision. Even so, in your work as a teacher, you will be called upon to play a limited role in helping your students with personal issues, mostly listening and supporting, occasionally making referrals to qualified experts. If you think you already have enough to do, you are right. In Asia and other cultures where there are no counselors in schools, teachers are called upon to serve in those roles in addition to other responsibilities. Furthermore, you could easily make a case that if a child does have a problem, the teacher is actually the one best positioned to intervene and is likely to be the initial adult in whom the child seeks to confide.

Although it is neither your job nor part of your training to do counseling, you will have numerous opportunities to make a significant impact on students' lives through the helping relationships you create with them. Being a teacher involves so much more than imparting wisdom and information; it means being available and accessible to students when personal issues are interfering with their ability to concentrate and excel in school.

What sorts of issues may come your way while you sit at your desk grading papers? The following is but a sampling:

- "Nobody ever wants to play with me. They always tease me and call me 'turtle brain.' Can I stay inside and help you today?"
- "There is this girl I like, sort of, but she won't talk to me."
- "Mrs. Rainey won't ever call on me. She thinks I'm stupid."
- "Nothing I do is ever good enough for my dad."
- "My uncle touches me sometimes, like in the middle of the night."
- "I don't know why I keep forgetting my homework."
- "Nobody ever picks me to play on their team."
- "My parents always nag me to clean up my room. That's all they ever do, nag, nag, nag."
- "Some of my friends think that I might be drinking a little too much. They think I should talk to somebody about it."
- "My mommy and daddy scream so much that it sometimes hurts my stomach."
- "How do you know if you're gay or not?"

In every one of these situations, you will be called upon to offer support and be caring, to be a good listener, and, most of all, to build trust. For you to offer this sense of comfort and nurture, children must feel that they are safe when talking to you.

Confidentiality

Being able to keep things private is another factor that makes helping relationships special. Doctors and lawyers are protected by laws of privileged communication that allow them to keep information private. Counselors and therapists also maintain confidentiality. Teachers, as well, are in a position to receive private information as they develop trust with children. They build a reputation for ensuring safety, for keeping communications private, and for keeping promises.

There are certain circumstances and times, of course, when you cannot maintain silence. In fact, in most states you are mandated by law to report suspected instances of physical or sexual abuse and neglect. Also, when you feel a child is likely to do something dangerous, in the form of hurting either self or others, you will be required to make a prompt report to authorities. For these reasons it is important never to promise a student you will keep what they are going to tell you a secret. In most instances, however, the problems that children will bring to you about friends and family, about fears and dreams, can and should be kept between the two of you.

Sometimes the best thing you can do to be helpful is to be perceived by students as someone in whom it is safe to confide. This is especially true if you refrain from giving advice when everyone in their lives is telling them what to do. Children, like all the rest of us, just want to feel heard and respected. They want to be understood by us without our needing to tell them what to do and how to do it so that we can feel less helpless. There will be times when students will want to confide in us things that make us feel uncomfortable, such as sex or religion. In these situations, you need to set limits and explain them to the student as you gently refer the student to someone else to talk to.

Empathy

The ability and willingness to step inside a child's shoes, to feel what the child is going through, to really know what it is like to be this child is what empathy is all about. Empathy involves even more than trying to imagine what a child is going through, however; it means also being a partner in the journey toward resolution of the problem. When you adopt an empathic posture, you are able to resonate with the child's pain and discomfort and, even more important, you are able to communicate this deep level of understanding.

It is this unconditional love and caring that is a primary impetus for children to feel better about themselves. After all, if you, their brilliant and wonderful teacher, can find them worthy of your love and care, then maybe, just maybe, *they* can begin to love themselves.

THE HELPING PROCESS

To encourage others to find you attractive and approachable, trustworthy and safe, there are several skills you can learn that are part of the overall helping process. These behaviors, adapted for teachers from counseling settings, form the basis of facilitating exploration, insight, and action in resolving personal problems. Table 5.1 presents the helping process as a sequential series of four stages, each of which builds on its antecedent. Each component of this methodology requires the mastery of a set of skills. As we review these helping skills, you may find it useful to consider your current levels of functioning in each of these dimensions. This self-assessment will aid you in your efforts to improve your interpersonal functioning by helping you to identify areas of personal strengths and weaknesses.

Assessment

In the first stage of the helping process, you listen and attend to the student so that you can accurately observe and hear what is being communicated. Your job is not to diagnose and fix problems that are presented to you; rather it is to help the children do this for themselves. The first and foremost set of skills that help you to hear what is being said, to collect relevant information about the presenting

Table 5.1   The Helping Process

Stage	Skills
1. Assessment	Attending Listening Focusing Observing
2. Exploration	Reflecting feelings Responding to content Probing, questioning Showing empathy
3. Understanding	Interpreting Confronting Challenging Giving information Self-disclosing
4. Action	Goal setting Role playing Reinforcing

complaint, and to make sense of what a person really means are called "attending behaviors." This process of active listening is not as easy as it sounds.

Before children even open their mouths, you first set in motion a series of internal adjustments inside your head that permit you to be receptive. In earlier chapters, we talked about the attitudes that help you to remain clear and neutral. This means clearing your mind of distractions—things you have done or will do later, a grumbling stomach, or things going on around you. To enter a helping process means making a commitment to giving a person your full attention without interruption. Sometimes this simple action, in itself, is experienced as healing by people with problems, because they just want a sounding board against which to bounce their ideas or feelings. This internal climate inside your head involves reminding yourself to stay nonjudgmental, to focus concentration, and to take that deep cleansing breath that keeps you centered.

In this initial stage of helping, you are attending both mentally and physically. You are not sitting behind a desk; on the contrary, you are doing everything you can to remove all barriers, physical or psychological, between you and the child. You are using eye contact, facial expressions, and body postures to communicate that this child to whom you are speaking is the most important person in the world to you at that moment in time. The child revels in your attention and feels nurtured by your soothing energy.

We invite you to experiment with these attending behaviors in your current personal relationships. During the next few days, pay particular attention to how you relate to your friends. Practice giving them your undivided attention. Use your eyes, body posture, head nods, and smiles to let them know you are hanging on their every word. Note what a difference such simple changes make in the quality and intimacy of your interactions.

You still have not opened your mouth or begun the interaction process, yet you are running through a mental checklist just the way a pilot would do before takeoff. You check your attitudes to make sure you are clearheaded, respectful, authentic, and compassionate. You heighten your sensitivity to what is unfolding by actually entering a meditative, altered state of consciousness that allows you to see and hear things just beneath the surface of ordinary reality.

This very state is what permits therapists to appear to read minds. Expert helpers have taught themselves to concentrate so intently on what is taking place that they are able to pick up cues that are invisible to the less informed. A child says, "I don't have a problem," but you hear a subtle nuance that tells you something different. A child's imperceptibly blinking eyes, flushed face, and quivering lip give valuable clues as to what is going on inside, signs that can be read and interpreted, given practice.

Most of the skills we are discussing in this chapter and the preceding ones cannot be learned by merely reading about them; you must find ways to practice them to the point where they become relatively natural. For each of the main helping areas, we thus present at the end of the discussion a self-assessment exercise that you can use to determine your current functioning in relation to where you would eventually like to be.

Self-Assessment–Attending Skills

Rate the items below on a scale of 1 to 5, evaluating your level of proficiency in each of the behaviors.

(5) All the time (4) Most of the time (3) Sometimes (2) Rarely (1) Never

☐ I am nonjudgmental and accepting of others who are different from me.

☐ I give people my full attention when listening.

☐ I demonstrate good eye contact and body position when attending to others.

☐ I am sensitive to and able to hear and observe subtleties in others' messages.

☐ I appear caring and authentic in my style of relating to others.

Check those items that you feel especially motivated to work on improving.

Exploration

When you have given students your full attention, they feel encouraged to tell you what is going on in their lives. Your job in this stage of helping is to gently facilitate the process of self-awareness. You can do this in a number of ways. In response to each statement a person makes, you have a variety of ways in which you can proceed. You can focus on the content of the communication and on the underlying feeling that is being expressed. For example, in the statement, "Teacher, will the test be hard?" a student is communicating a content-oriented question (which can be answered with a yes or no), as well as an underlying feeling (anxiety, apprehension, fear, or confidence). During this phase, you are listening carefully to what the student is saying, observing and then attempting to help the student to make sense of what is being said. You are applying the skills of active listening, mentioned in the previous chapter, in a more focused manner.

You are relying on three main skills during this interaction. First, *reflection of feeling*—you feed back to the student the underlying emotion that you hear expressed:

Student: I know that no matter how hard I study I'll just never pass this course.

Teacher: You feel so frustrated—just like a failure. You seriously wonder whether you will get credit for the course.

This intervention accomplishes several tasks simultaneously: (a) You act as a mirror, reflecting the essence of what you heard expressed; this helps the students clarify what they are experiencing inside. (b) You prove that you not only heard the student but also really understood. (c) You are able to check the accuracy of what you heard. The beauty of this intervention is that even when your reflection is not accurate, the student is encouraged to clarify further:

Student: Well, not exactly. It's not that I feel like a failure as much as that I don't want to disappoint my parents.

The student has therefore articulated more clearly the real issue here. Even when your reflections fall short of the mark, the student is still encouraged to look inside to clarify what is felt, thought, and experienced. As beginners, you can feel some relief that as long as you avoid giving people advice and telling them what to do with their lives, you will not do harm even if you do not help them. This principle should be a major consideration in your helping efforts.

Exploration is further encouraged through a second and parallel skill, *reflection of content.*

Student: You see, my older brother can do no wrong in my parents' eyes. It's me they jump all over.

Teacher: You are tired of being the focus all the time.

Restating the students' content is also helpful in letting them know that you are hearing accurately what was said, which facilitates further the flow of communication. You thus have two means to foster deeper exploration, reflecting either the content of what was said or the underlying feeling that you sense. Because it is so difficult to decode meaning and formulate an appropriate response in the 2-second pause you have between verbalizations, you are likely to rely mostly on paraphrasing (reflections of content), occasionally inserting reflections of feeling as you get a sense of what might be happening beneath the surface.

Let us see what this looks and sounds like during an interaction between a teacher and a student upset about his grade on an assignment. Notice that throughout this dialogue the teacher refrains from becoming defensive or even asking any questions. Instead, she just keeps putting the ball back in the student's court, letting him sort things out for himself as he gets clearer about his thoughts and feelings.

Student: You gave me the wrong grade on my assignment.

Teacher: You're wondering whether I made a mistake because this grade is unexpected. (Reflection of content)

Student: Yeah! I mean, I worked hard on this project.

Teacher: (Stalling) You really put a lot of effort into it.

Student: You got that right!

Teacher: (Stalling) Um huh. (Verbal encouragement and nonverbal attending)

Student: So, what are you going to do about this mistake?

Teacher: You're thinking I made a mistake, and you're hoping I'll change your grade. (Reflection of content)

Student: Will you?

Teacher: I can tell that you're really upset about this. (Ignores question and reflects underlying feeling)

Student: Are you kidding? You know what my dad's going to do when he sees this? He'll kill me.

Teacher: This is more than just a grade on an assignment to you. There's a lot at stake.

With just a little bit of effort, the teacher has ignored the temptation to defend her actions or to solve the problem and instead simply reflects back what she hears. Or rather, it is not simple at all; she digs deep, listening to what is being expressed and communicating back what she hears.

We warn you that these skills are especially difficult for teachers to master, because of the preference for solving problems as soon as possible rather than taking the time to explore the situation fully. It also helps to remember that it is not your job to fix things but rather to allow students the opportunity to resolve their own difficulties.

A third useful skill you can employ in this stage of the helping process involves the use of a few well-placed questions. These questions should usually be *open-ended* rather than *closed-ended* ones which can be answered yes or no. Note the difference between the following two questions:

Closed-ended question: Do you feel pressure at home?

Open-ended question: How do you feel about what is going on at home?

Open-ended questions are phrased in such a way as to encourage students to elaborate on their experiences. They draw people out in a style in which they do not feel interrogated but rather gently prodded to share more about themselves. Along with reflections of feeling and of content, such questions help the student to explore exactly what is going on as a precursor to developing some understanding of the problem.

Self-Assessment–Exploration Skills

Rate the items on a scale of 1 to 5, evaluating your level of proficiency in each of the behaviors.

(5) All the time (4) Most of the time (3) Sometimes (2) Rarely (1) Never

☐ I am sensitive to other people's feelings.

☐ I am good at getting people to open up and express themselves.

☐ People tell me I am a good listener.

☐ People seem to trust me and confide in me.

Check those items that you feel especially motivated to work on improving.

Understanding

Exploration logically and naturally leads to greater self-awareness and understanding. Before people can change some aspect of themselves, it is usually desirable for them to understand (a) how the problem developed, (b) when and where the problem is worse, (c) exceptions to when the problem is operative, and (d) other areas of life to which the problem is related. All of these factors are crucial to later action stages.

This phase of helping can often be quite complex, even beyond the limits of what a teacher, even a skilled helper, can do in a few sessions. Sometimes many months of lengthy sessions are required by the expert counselor or therapist to help the child uncover the source of problems or the underlying conflicts. For example, Raul, an otherwise well-behaved child who suddenly begins acting out in class, may not know what is bothering him or why he is acting so obnoxiously. He may not even be motivated to change if the symptoms are serving some apparently useful purpose to him. It may take the experienced counselor quite some time to get to the bottom of the problem.

In this case, Raul began acting out at school about the same time his parents escalated their fighting with one another. As long as he was identified as a "problem child," the parents would stop bickering with one another and would show a unified front to try to help him. Once he would straighten out, the parents would then resume their war. Although this was beyond his conscious awareness, Raul had found a way to keep his parents' marriage together. This illustrates the limits of what even an expert helper can do without involving the whole family in counseling. It also highlights the more realistic goal of the teacher/helper—to listen, provide support, and then make appropriate referrals.

There are many instances, however, when in a few sessions together, the teacher can help to promote some degree of insight by applying a variety of skills. *Interpretation* is the attempt to uncover the underlying meaning of a pattern of behavior. *Confrontation,* when used carefully and diplomatically, can also be extremely useful in pointing out discrepancies between what people say they want versus what they do. Both of these interventions (along with others you have already learned) are evident in the following dialogue with Raul:

Teacher: What can I help you with? (Open-ended question) You look upset about something. (Reflection of feeling)

Raul: Oh, it's probably nothing.

Teacher: You are saying it's not that important, but it seems you are concerned about something that you want to talk about. (Reflection of content)

Raul: I don't know why I act like such a smart-ass in your class. I just can't help it.

Teacher: One reason may be related to something you mentioned earlier when you said your parents acted so much nicer to one another when they were angry with you. (Interpretation)

Raul: Well, that's sorta true, I guess.

Teacher: You sound hesitant about that now, and a little scared about what that might mean if it was true. (Reflection of feeling)

Raul: Nah. I just don't think it's that big a deal.

Teacher: Let me know if this doesn't fit, but I'm a little confused. Just a few minutes ago, you were saying this was *a very* big deal, maybe the biggest deal in your life at this time. But now you're saying it doesn't matter. (Confrontation) It sounds like you are having some doubts about looking at this too deeply. (Reflection of content and feeling)

In this 2-minute conversation, quite a lot was learned and explored. Given Raul's ambivalence and hesitance about getting too far into this, it might very well be best to end the talk at this point, resuming at another time. It is often the case that you will not have very much time in your helping interactions with kids, a few minutes here and there. That is fine, because it does not take very long to communicate your continuing interest and concern for those who are having a hard time.

Self-Assessment–Insight Skills

(5) All the time (4) Most of the time (3) Sometimes (2) Rarely (1) Never

Rate the items on a scale of 1 to 5, evaluating your level of proficiency in each of the behaviors.

- ☐ I am patient in helping others to go at their own pace.

- ☐ I spend time reflecting on the meaning of my own behavior.

- ☐ I am willing to disclose aspects of my life in an effort to help people feel closer to me.

- ☐ I confront people in a nonthreatening way.

- ☐ I am good at figuring out the hidden motives behind people's behavior.

Check those items that you feel especially motivated to work on improving.

Action

Helping students to understand how and why they have difficulties can be useful but often is not enough. There are some people walking around who are severely dysfunctional, who understand why they are so messed up, but who still refuse to change in any fundamental way. Helping students to translate their insights into some form of action is thus crucial to constructive change.

In its simplest form, this stage can be initiated by asking the student, "So, what do you intend to do about your situation?" This places responsibility squarely on the child's shoulders and implies that (a) something can be done, and (b) it is up to the child to do it. The objective of this phase is to help students set realistic goals, create a plan to reach them, and then secure a commitment to follow through with what is intended.

Kim feels stymied in her efforts to make more friends, but she is determined to keep trying. She reaches out to her teacher for support. In a previous talk, she had the opportunity to express her anger and frustration and feelings of loneliness. She then felt safe enough to explore with her teacher what she might be doing to turn people off.

Teacher: Last time you talked about how difficult it is to make new friends since you moved to this school. How do you feel about _____?

Kim: I understand that sometimes I do come on too strong. And you're right the way you pointed out how I tend to reject kids before they can reject me. I would like to try doing things differently. Maybe I could be a little more agreeable the next time kids approach me instead of scaring them away.

The skill of effective goal setting is the method by which you can help children to create objectives that meet the following criteria:

1. They should be specific and describe in detail exactly what will be done, when it will be done, and how often it will be repeated.

2. They should be realistic and attainable objectives that can be reasonably completed within time limits. Make sure that kids do not bite off more than they can chew.

3. They should be mutually negotiated rather than prescribed by you. The last thing students want from a teacher is another homework assignment. It is far better to encourage students to declare what they would like to do. That way, if the goal is not completed, it is the student's choice rather than a reaction to your intervention.

In the following conversation, a teacher is helping a second-grade child to work on some constructive action to overcome his chronic shyness:

Teacher: You were saying that it's not that you're shy in all situations, but just in school.

Student: Well, sometimes.

Teacher: You mean that there are times here in school when you aren't shy as well. For instance, you were telling me that when you are playing soccer during recess you're one of the first kids picked to play on a team.

Student: (Smiles) Yeah.

Teacher: You've also said that you'd like to do something about this problem. So, what do you want to do?

Student: (Shrugs)

Teacher: You're not sure what to do.

Student: I guess I could start talking more. Like in class and stuff.

Teacher: That's a great idea, but how could you go about doing that, because it's been so hard for you?

Student: Well, like in your class, I could talk more.

Teacher: Okay. Let's start small with some little steps in the direction you'd like to go.

In this conversation, you will recognize the teacher using all of the preceding skills you have learned. First, the issue is clarified, and the child's thoughts and feelings on the matter are labeled and reflected back to him. Resisting the urge to tell the student what to do (and often we think we know what will work best), the teacher instead slowly leads the child to declare his own course of action that will help him to act less shyly.

In the action stage of helping, your objective is to encourage students to plan ways in which they would like to be different. Your job is to talk them through the process of generating alternatives, narrowing the choices to a preferred course of action, and following through with the plan. Often, role playing and other rehearsal strategies can be especially useful in building confidence and giving the child practice experimenting with new behaviors in a safe environment. For example, a teacher might suggest, "You say that you are tired of waiting for boys to ask you out and that you would like to be the one to initiate relationships. Pretend that I am a boy you like. How would you approach me?"

Self-Assessment–Action Skills

Rate the items on a scale of 1 to 5, evaluating your level of proficiency in each of the behaviors.

(5) All the time (4) Most of the time (3) Sometimes (2) Rarely (1) Never

- ☐ I am good at setting goals for myself and completing them.
- ☐ I am described by others as a "doer" rather than just a "talker."
- ☐ I am creative in solving problems.
- ☐ I am good at motivating people to follow through on tasks.

Check those items that you feel especially motivated to work on improving.

In addition to skills you have in helping children think through problems, find solutions, and carry them out; through your support and encouragement, you bring the helping process full circle back to the trust you established in the beginning. For although being a helper means that you are highly skilled in relationship building, communication, and problem solving, the essence of the process involves being perceived as trustworthy and safe to confide in. Supporting students to take action, from your perspective, particularly as a new teacher, may be for the students to get help from a professional.

WINDOW INTO A CLASSROOM

Being an effective helper to your students requires not only knowledge and skills of appropriate interventions and a helping process; it also demands acute sensitivity to the individual and social contexts of their lives. As we mentioned previously, one of the settings for helping a student can occur in a conference with the child's parents.

On one memorable occasion, the parents of a fifth-grade boy were referred to me (S. Z.) at a university where I was a professor of reading and language arts. They came to my office for several visits while we began the process of assessing, exploring, and understanding the learning needs of their son, John. I'll never forget the shame and helplessness of John's parents, both university professors, as they recounted his school problems.

They told me that John had been socially promoted each year to the next grade, although he was unable to read, write, compute, or make substantial progress in any academic area. The only success John found in school was in beating up other kids, a behavior for which he was punished and regularly kept indoors during recess and in isolation during class time. His parents were mortified by John's behavior. He had been moved from one elementary school to another in the college town where they lived, and he was on the notorious list of disruptive elementary students. His parents were desperate in their attempts to find remedial assistance and counseling for their son.

John, however, wanted nothing to do with any kind of help. During our first meeting, he had to be literally dragged into my office by his father, who was reluctant to leave him alone with me because of fear for my safety. In my initial weekly sessions with John, I knew I had to establish a context different from ones in which he had experienced continuous school failure.

In the early stages of assessing John's emotional and literacy needs, I discovered amid all the debris of anger and shattered self-esteem one source of hope. Unknown to his teachers and his classmates was one small, private area of competence. John was a bicycle racing superstar. In the context of our individual meetings, John taught me more than I ever hoped to know about racing bikes. His self-esteem grew as he assisted me in learning how to repair and maintain my own bike. The praise and admiration I gave him was not feigned or insincere. He seemed to be a living example of what Gardner (1993, 1999) has identified as multiple intelligences. He might not excel in the classroom, but this kid was a wizard at mechanical skills and street smarts.

John gradually opened up to my exploration of his feelings and helped us to understand his frustrations. One day, as we sat in my office at the beginning of our session, I got a call from his mother. She told me that she had forgotten to give John money to ride the bus from his school to our campus. "Pardon me a second," I said as I turned to John. "This is your mother, John; she didn't think you'd be here today."

"I know," John replied, "she forgot to give me bus money this morning. I had to use my lunch money." At that moment, I knew John was ready for action.

John dictated a book to me, *Ten-Speed Bicycle Maintenance.* He carefully described each step of the maintenance and repair process, and I wrote down the steps. He knew big words such as *lubrication;* he even knew French words such as *derailleur.* Over the weeks, John learned to read the book he had written. Playing catch-up, John wrote another book, *Fun Ten-Speed Bicycle Trips.*

There was one more context in which John needed help before he could make the kind of academic progress in school that he so desperately wanted. Before students with learning difficulties, such as John, can achieve academic success in the classroom, another helping intervention must be enacted.

Students with high academic status effectively prevent others from finding success through such subtle tactics as shunning and name calling. In fact, John had been called dummy and airhead so often he believed these labels defined who he was. The interventions John's teachers and I used to help these bright students become more tolerant and accepting of John involved a reversal of high-status roles. John read his books to his classmates. We put his books in the school library, where many of his classmates could read them and examine his excellent illustrations. Finally, in the context of the whole class, the most effective intervention in changing the attitude of John's peers was found when John assisted his classmates in acquiring the skills they needed to repair and maintain their own bicycles. John became an effective helper; John's teachers became more effective helpers, too.

We present this case example to you, not just as an object lesson of the work you can do, but rather as an illustration of how any helping effort must occur in the context of the child's world. That is one reason why individual counseling is now often being replaced by group and family interventions that examine the underlying "systemic" forces that control behavior. No matter how much success you encounter during individual conferences, if the child returns to the same dysfunctional family or peer group, all your efforts may be minimized or neutralized.

It is beyond the scope of your job, as well as your training, to plan and implement a series of interventions similar to those described above. Besides, you do not have the time or the energy to schedule regular sessions with kids on an ongoing basis; that, after all, is what professional counselors and therapists are for. But there is so much you *can* do to help children experience good helping relationships, to offer support and encouragement, and to get them started on a path toward greater success and satisfaction. In such instances, your referrals are more likely to "stick," meaning that kids are more inclined to follow your suggestions and seek the help they need. You have shown them that adults can be trusted, and they can treat children with respect. Remember: It all starts with your helping attitudes and relationships. This is especially true when you can apply what you know to your own life to prolong your career in the teaching profession and prevent the insidious forms of stress that so often cause burnout.

BEYOND THE CLASSROOM

Veteran teachers often begin to move into new roles in the school where helping skills will be especially important. Whether a department chair, a supervising teacher for a student teacher, a mentor, or teacher leader for professional development in a particular subject, these skills will serve you well as you interact with your colleagues. Whether you assume these roles formally or informally, they will provide fresh, exciting opportunities for you to utilize your expertise and further grow professionally.

SUGGESTED ACTIVITIES

1. Interview school counselors on the types of problems that are commonly referred to their office.

2. With a partner, take turns asking open-ended questions as you explore how each of you feels about an issue.

3. Identify a problem you are experiencing and apply the strategies described in this chapter: explore the issue, identify possible solutions, select a course of action, evaluate the effectiveness of your choice. Practice implementing this way of approaching problems in the future.

CHAPTER SIX

On Struggling With the Challenges of the Profession

Teaching, like any other profession, has its own unique set of challenges. Many of these challenges (we prefer not to label them "problems") exist because teaching and learning are rooted in the human dimension. That means that we do not always act rationally, even when it might be in our best interests to do so. Likewise, schools are not entirely rational institutions; they are neither designed nor run with the efficiency and effectiveness that would be desired. In addition, there are many other challenges we face with a lack of resources, overcrowded classes, unmotivated students, uninvolved or over-involved parents, unsupportive colleagues, insensitive administrators, and so on.

SOURCES OF STRESS IN A TEACHER'S LIFE

Although you may prefer to imagine that most of the obstacles you will face result from external factors outside your control, this is not strictly the case. Teachers experience stress from a number of sources, including the following main areas:

1. *What others do to you.* Difficult students, incompetent administrators, backbiting colleagues, uncooperative parents, and unsupportive friends or family can all be a source of stress.

2. *What the environment does to you.* The politics, conflicted relationships, chaos, negative attitudes around you, and less-than-desirable physical space contribute to stress levels.

3. *What the job does to you.* There is too little time and too much to do. You are on your feet nonstop throughout the day. Even finding time for a bathroom break is a challenge, much less time to catch your breath. Everyone wants a piece of your hide.

4. *What you do to yourself.* Your own unrealistic expectations, fears of failure, self-doubts and insecurities, negative attitudes, and irrational thinking create your own needless suffering.

Interestingly, it is really the last category that you are in a position to do the most about. You cannot make your administrators or colleagues change their behavior, as much as you might like to make that happen. You are not in a position to alter the economic realities of your district budget or school resources. You have little control over things like the schedule, workload, and class size. You cannot even choose the students you prefer to teach.

Rather than dwelling on what you cannot do much about, you assuredly *can* deal with the problems you create for yourself. You are in control of your own lifestyle, including the ways you eat, rest, relax, and diversify your life and who you choose to hang out with. Just as important, you are in charge of what you think inside your own head and how you choose to look at your situation. You can treat the challenges you face as mere inconveniences and annoying obstacles or you can blow them way out of proportion and totally demoralize yourself. The difference is often a matter of subtleties in the ways you look at your work and your situation.

In the next chapter on preventing burnout, we will talk a lot more about ways to handle challenges and sources of stress; for now, let us peer into the classroom—and the mind—of one teacher who has managed to stay on top of the challenges she has faced.

WINDOW INTO A CLASSROOM

Gwen, a veteran teacher, is late for school but not because she overslept. In fact, she got up at the crack of dawn so that she could finish grading a stack of papers that students are waiting for with apprehension. It seems that throughout the school year, she feels as though she can never quite catch up with all the demands that are placed upon her—by her principal, her department head, her colleagues, the students in her classes, their parents, her own family and friends. Even the custodian has expectations that she will maintain her classroom in a particular way. Sometimes she forgets what she wants in her own life because she is so used to taking care of everyone else.

Gwen feels that the most important part of her job is to stay fresh and energized when working with children. She tries to demonstrate the creativity and passion for learning that she considers such an important part of her teaching style. The problem for her is how to maintain such a high degree of commitment and excitement for what she is doing when she has 6 different classes to prepare for each day, 131 students to work with, and only 45-minute blocks of time in which to do it. She also struggles with balancing the need to finish the prescribed curriculum and provide depth of learning as well. Sometimes the curriculum appears to be a river a mile wide and a half inch deep.

Furthermore, it is difficult for Gwen to reconcile the requirements of her school district with her actual love of teaching. Between the achievement tests she must administer, the daily discipline problems, the lack of resources available to her, and the meddling by some administrators and parents, she wonders how any learning takes place at all. During those admittedly rare magical days when she feels she has gotten through to her students about something really important, she wonders whether her efforts will ultimately make much of a difference. After all, as soon as the children walk out of her class, they enter the worlds of others who inadvertently or deliberately sabotage her efforts. The children are condemned to serve sentences in the classrooms of some colleagues who at best are boring and at worst, downright incompetent. What they will remember about school is not the fun they had learning in her class but the abuse they suffered at the hands of others. Then, once out of class, those who really like to learn and want to study are ridiculed by their peers. Worst of all, so many of the children go home to families that are deprived or dysfunctional, it is a wonder they can survive at all.

Gwen thinks about one student in particular. Dino comes from what you might describe as a "conflicted" family. When he was six years old, one of his older brothers killed his younger sister because she would not stop crying. At the time, their mother lay passed out in the bedroom, where she sometimes camps out for days at a time. There is no place at home, or in his whole neighborhood, where Dino can find any privacy for his studies. He could be an outstanding student (and does perform brilliantly during Gwen's class), but he is repeatedly disillusioned by his experiences at home and with several other teachers who are somewhat less than captivating. Lately, Dino has been prone to acting out in Gwen's class as well, so she wonders whether all the time and effort she has devoted to handling him with special care means anything at all.

What Gwen likes best about her job is the power she has to influence the growth and learning of young, impressionable minds. This brings her a great sense of pride and accomplishment. What Gwen likes least about her job is the powerlessness she feels in having her efforts repeatedly undermined by factors that are completely out of her control: (a) children's attitudes about education that have been shaped by others; (b) children's often less-than-encouraging peer groups and family environments; (c) administrators and colleagues who are not as supportive as she would like them to be; (d) a less-than-ideal school environment; and (e) endless paperwork—papers and tests to grade, homework to check, lesson plans to file, reports to complete, assessments to administer. A major theme in Gwen's professional life as a teacher is sometimes feeling so powerful when she can see some child change in a fundamental way, and yet feeling so powerless to facilitate this result more often. The struggles that Gwen, the veteran teacher, seeks to balance in her professional life are similar to the challenges facing beginning teachers in schools everywhere, whether they are public or private, urban or rural, at-risk, or affluent.

The situation for teachers is complex. On the one hand, we have a group of professionals who, like most human beings, need to feel in control of their lives; on the other hand, the school environment is often designed (or at least has evolved) in such a way that teachers report feeling so powerless. Because students feel much the same way, the whole atmosphere is permeated with this sense of helplessness. Reform movements today are addressing these issues by providing opportunities for teachers to work together to analyze achievement data and student needs, determine needed resources, and implement effective, research-based best practices; to give input into the design of their professional development; and, to increase parental or guardian and community involvement in schools.

REAL VERSUS IDEAL

In an ideal world, teachers would be greatly appreciated and rewarded appropriately for their worth as the guardians of society's greatest resource—children's impressionable minds. We would have unlimited resources with which to work our wonders and would be able to do so in optimal learning environments that are attractive, stimulating, and comfortable. We would have adequate support staff in the form of consultants, aides, counselors, and administrators. The parents of our children would be our greatest allies, supporting our efforts, magnifying our lessons at home, encouraging their children to be eager consumers of our valuable services. We would have all the resources we desire: state-of-the-art, multimedia computers, support technology, books, artifacts, and supplementary materials.

Most of all, in this ideal world, we would teach students who are eager and highly motivated to learn. They would be well fed, well clothed, and well nurtured at home. They would be polite, cooperative, and well behaved. They would show us great respect because of our exalted positions as teachers, the imparters of wisdom. Of course, they would be hungry to know everything we have to offer and yet still beg us for more. Discipline would certainly not be a problem, because they would view the opportunity to attend school as a privilege.

Furthermore, central administration and our own principal would have utmost trust in our competence. Money would be available for all the inservice training, supervision, and professional development that we could desire. Paperwork, lesson plans, self-evaluations, and annual reviews would be kept to a minimum (or completed by aides), so that we could do what teachers do best: help children learn.

Well, you only have to compare this ideal world of education to that of everyday schooling to get a gigantic dose of reality. Perhaps now you get a sense of the struggle that many teachers face in confronting their own sense of powerlessness. Once upon a time, they felt sure they could set the world on fire, just like you. Then, they faced the realities of teaching. Many of their children were so under-privileged, unmotivated, disadvantaged, and distracted that performing well in school was their absolute last priority. Not infrequently, teachers feel completely at a loss as to what to do when they stand in front of a class where students are bickering and throwing things across the room, while the most well-behaved students are withdrawn and maybe even dozing with heads down at their desks. Then, if by some miracle these teachers can attract and maintain the students' attention, how are they to communicate when the students either do not speak English or have limited English skills? How are they to make personal connections when there are over 40 students in a classroom and not even enough seats to go around? And, what happens after the class is over? What is the likelihood that their students will do any homework or preparation for the next day? How will they ever prepare students for all the mandated achievement tests when many lack the prerequisite skills and knowledge expected of students at their grade levels?

The good news is teachers do not have to answer all these questions simultaneously. They acknowledge the areas in which they have control, set goals, seek answers, and address issues as they arise to the best of their ability with support from colleagues.

For those who were impressed with the short work day and school year calendar, we need to point out the demands for a teacher's time extend beyond the school day. Parent conferences and IEP (individualized education plan) meetings may occur before or after school or during a preparation period. Department meetings, faculty meetings, and district curriculum meetings are generally held after school. Professional development programs, while often held during the day with released time provided by a substitute, are also offered after school and during the summer so teachers won't have to leave their classes. Teachers need time to consult with colleagues to improve their practice and continually upgrade technology skills. Additionally, for the first one or two years, new teachers are typically required to participate in induction programs. Veteran teachers often become mentors or supervising teachers for university student teachers. All teachers are constantly asked to lead after school programs for remediation and clubs or coach sports. Evening programs include Back to School Night, Open House, and Family Nights for mathematics, science, history, geography or other subjects. Although the timing is flexible, teachers grade papers, prepare lessons, request supplies, complete progress reports after school or on the weekends.

As a result, teachers carefully plan their calendars and guard their schedules so as not to commit themselves to the point they feel overwhelmed with obligations.

Even as teacher salaries are slowly increasing (Ryan & Cooper, 2004), we could in no way describe the compensation as generous. That is one reason why so many teachers attempt to supplement their income with other work: teaching summer school, substituting when they are "off track," sponsoring clubs, or coaching sports. Others choose to write curriculum and assessments for their districts for additional pay. Some consider going back to the university to get additional degrees with the benefit of also advancing on the salary scale. Although there are many benefits from these activities, ranging from involvement with colleagues to financial gains, they serve as extra demands on one's time and energy. Teachers need to carefully evaluate their lifestyle choices.

Family and friends need to be aware of your commitments to educating youth and your contributions to your students and their community. They can be a source of encouragement and support for you when energy wanes and disappointments occur. They can share in the joys and accomplishments as well.

We do not mean to discourage those of you who are beginning or future teachers, or in any way temper your enthusiasm about doing things differently; we just want you to realize what you are up against—aging schools with limited resources, diversity of student populations, limited language abilities of students, instructional days lost to testing, political battles, obstacles that you must overcome if you ever hope to thrive in this profession. For every burned-out, despondent teacher who feels powerless, there is another one who has developed the inner resources to retain a sense of potency, even in the face of annoying and inconvenient problems. In fact, such teachers even prefer to treat obstacles or problems as challenges that can be overcome with a little patience, fortitude, and ingenuity.

Yes, it would be wonderful to work in a school where you are empowered by the principal, the parents, and the system to work effectively as a teacher. Suppose, however, that you are not one of these fortunate ones. Moreover, let us assume that your work environment is fraught with obstacles and is sometimes downright hostile. In the following section, we share some strategies you can employ to help you maintain your idealism and enthusiasm for teaching and learning even in such a challenging environment.

Window Into a Classroom

Ray is respected by his high school colleagues, as well as the student grapevine, as being a competent, dedicated teacher. His students describe him as a "together guy," who "really cares about us as people." In spite of his well-deserved reputation, Ray gets little support from the administration in his impossible assignment of making competent, sensitive writers out of his 150 students. In fact, the principal observes him for about 5 minutes a year; gives him a swift, superficial evaluation; and praises him for maintaining effective control of his students. The principal rarely makes any acknowledgment of the fact that Ray is an effective teacher.

What are the sources for Ray's success as a teacher? One of the factors is revealed in the assessment his students give him. He possesses a strong identity built on a genuine feeling of self-worth. He has learned that his true identity is built on a number of self images: the images of husband, father, friend, teacher, writer, poet, individual, and risk taker. He recognizes that he continues to construct additional images of himself based on the new experiences, new people, and new places he encounters in his life.

Although Ray recognizes these new images of his dynamic, developing identity, he also takes comfort in an inner core of his being that remains grounded. This inner core provides Ray with a personal meaning that empowers him as a satisfied, integral person. At one time in his life, he searched outside of himself for peace, happiness, and joy. His search ended after much personal pain and despair, when he found he had the power to find the peace, joy, and happiness he longed for within his own being.

Ray is a fully functioning human being who knows how to flex his individual self to accommodate the rigid demands of the environment in which he lives and works. This flexibility provides him with a subtle but conscious control over many aspects of his workaday world. He may bend, but he does not break.

Ray sets reasonable goals and takes pride in what he is able to accomplish in the classroom. He carefully builds relationships with students throughout the year, recognizing that this process takes time and effort. He works to establish a comfortable environment in the classroom where his students will feel safe asking questions by providing them opportunities to get to know each other in risk-free ways—by interviewing each other and working in small groups to complete structured tasks. He is quick to end any form of harassment, such as ridicule. He asks his students to share their writing with each other, and he also reads them examples of his own work. He praises them for their accomplishments and helps them to recognize the progress they make throughout the year. He would like to reach all students, but he knows some will be beyond his grasp.

Inside the classroom, Ray has bookshelves and cabinets for his materials giving an organized feel to the space. Rules and a few motivational sayings are posted along with writing guides. On one side of the room, space is provided for a "word wall" for all the new words students are learning this year. Also on the walls, you will find projects and samples of all the students' writing. He would like to have new computers in his room, but he knows that is unlikely this year and probably the next, so he does the best he can without them. Outside the room, Ray spends time in the hall chatting with students about their lives outside of school, what television they watch, what movies they like, and what's going on in the community.

Ray sees the area of his room as his domain; he personalizes it and provides a welcome environment, physically, emotionally, and socially for his students. Those who come for help with homework, he can usually support; those who come with difficult personal problems, he refers to others, maybe another teacher, maybe the nurse, maybe a counselor, maybe a social worker. He is pleased that some students choose to confide in him, yet realizes not all will choose to do so.

ENDING ON A POSITIVE NOTE

Let us end this chapter by placing the challenges in perspective and examining what motivates people to go into teaching as a profession. If asked what led you on this path of being a teacher, you might respond with something similar to the following statements:

- "I love children. I've always liked being around kids. In fact, I feel more comfortable around them than I do most adults."
- "When I was struggling as a kid, one of my teachers was really there for me. She listened and supported me when nobody else believed in me. I want to pay her back by helping others like me."

- "I get a kick out of seeing people do new things on their own. It feels like such a privilege that I can be part of that growth."
- "What I do best in this life is learn. I'm captivated by learning. It is natural for me to want to model what I do best for my students!"
- "There are lots of callings in life, but none, I believe, as high as the profession of a teacher."
- "I want to make a difference in the world. I want to feel that I have helped to make things better."

It is this last statement that is at the heart of most teachers' motives. There is a wonderful sense of power in knowing that you have made a difference in someone's life, that if it were not for your efforts, a small part of the world would be worse off. It is the power to influence others that is so attractive to many of us who chose to be teachers. We giggle at the prospect of introducing some novel idea to children that we just know will change the way they see themselves or others. We feel dizzy with glee after getting through to someone who had previously been unreachable.

In her study of outstanding teachers who have stayed in the classroom over 15 years, Williams (2003) observed that exemplary educators are not motivated by external rewards or the hunger for power and prestige. Rather, most often, they describe the ways they have been able to express their creativity and autonomy in the classroom. They prize their meaningful relationships with students and colleagues. Most of all, they *know* they are making a difference in young people's lives.

PROFESSIONAL EFFICACY

We began this chapter with a description of what teachers struggle with most of their professional lives: power and powerlessness. In the final analysis, the focus on power issues in our profession comes down to one question: "Can I make a genuine difference in the lives of my students?" A teacher who possesses a strong sense of self worth will not hesitate to give an emphatic response to this question: "Of course, I want to make a genuine difference in the lives of my students! I genuinely care about them. I want them to succeed as students, as persons, and as productive citizens." Think about the many ways you can make a difference in the lives of your students.

Of course, there will be factors beyond your control that you will find frustrating in the teaching profession. Nevertheless, the degree to which you keep in touch with the many ways in which you make a difference in the lives of your students, a difference they would not experience if not for you, will give you the power to be an effective teacher. This power, in turn, will give you the daily energy you will need to avoid "going on automatic pilot" and experiencing burnout.

SUGGESTED ACTIVITIES

1. Participate in activities, whether paid or volunteer, to familiarize yourself with children and make sure you enjoy being around young people. Consider tutoring, serving as an aide, camp or recreational counseling, or coaching a sports team.

2. Observe master teachers to see how they skillfully handle their many responsibilities each day and how they meet the needs of their diverse students.

3. With a partner, discuss how you see yourself maintaining enthusiasm and energy in the classroom in light of the demands placed on teachers today.

4. Write a journal entry on your motivations for teaching. Examine your intrinsic and extrinsic motivations for entering the teaching profession.

CHAPTER SEVEN

On Avoiding Burnout and Rustout

> *Two teachers are leaving the school building after a long day. One looks haggard, his features drawn, his posture stooped. He shuffles toward his car carrying a huge backpack filled with books and materials. He stops for a minute to catch his breath, rearranges the straps of the heavy bag, and then continues onward with a deep sigh, as if he is not sure he wants to take another step forward, but certainly has no desire to go back where he came from.*
>
> *By contrast, the second teacher has a definite spring to her step. Once she says good-bye to her dispirited colleague, she practically breaks out in a spontaneous skip. She is more than 10 years older than her fellow teacher but looks quite a bit younger. She, too, stops for a moment, but as she looks over her shoulder back at the school, she starts to smile, remembering what happened during the day.*

How is it that two teachers, who do pretty much the same job, sharing identical responsibilities, and working with the same population of students, can react so differently to what they have experienced? The first teacher leaves each day feeling utterly exhausted and run down. When he returns the next morning, he will still be operating with the emotional and physical deficit that has been accumulating for years. The second teacher, however, feels absolutely invigorated as she launches herself out of school into her world. She feels great about what happened during her day and just as good about what is waiting for her at home.

The ways that teachers tend to deal with the challenges they face and metabolize the stresses they encounter depend on a number of factors, most of which are potentially within their control. Some teachers, like the first one, seem unable to control their workload and find it difficult to set and enforce limits on other people's demands of them. They are often discouraged and demoralized, sometimes even embittered. They are not much fun for their friends and family, and especially their students, to be around. Other teachers seem to find ways to take things in stride, to immunize themselves against the inevitable toxic elements that inhabit schools. They not only manage challenges that others find daunting, but even flourish because of them. Which teacher would *you* like to be?

AN OCCUPATIONAL HAZARD

In almost every people-oriented profession, from medicine to law enforcement, from social work to teaching, you will find a common malady with universal symptoms suffered by these diverse practitioners. *Burnout* is a professional hazard characterized by the following symptoms, as originally described by Maslach (1982) in her book on the consequences of caring:

1. A reluctance to discuss one's work with others

2. A high incidence of escapist daydreaming

3. Attitudes of cynicism, negativity, and callousness toward one's clients

4. Loss of enthusiasm for work

5. Emotional exhaustion and feelings of being used up

6. Decreased effectiveness in job performance

7. Blaming others for one's current unhappiness

8. Feeling powerless to alter one's situation

Maslach concludes by defining this condition as a time of emotional depletion and reduced satisfaction, when there is tremendous strain dealing with others in the workplace.

Burnout was first identified by Freudenberger (1974) when he observed that those who work in professions that demand high degrees of dedication and commitment to people are most vulnerable to this condition. Burnout is a form of occupational stress that is an inevitable struggle for all helping professionals who work with others, no matter how dedicated, committed, and skillful they may be.

From your perspective right now, filled as you are with excitement and enthusiasm for the profession of teaching, it may be difficult for you to imagine a time when you will feel listless, drained, and even despondent about your work with children. Is it inevitable that these demoralizing feelings will someday infect your professional life and damage your idealism? Is there nothing you can do to prevent the negative results of this occupational hazard or, at least, to minimize their destructive results?

Finding the answers to these questions is especially important early in your career, so that you may take steps to prepare yourself for the challenges you will face. Although feeling demoralized periodically may be normal and predictable, it is not inevitable that these feelings have to last very long. It is definitely not the case that you will have to surrender to them.

Although we have been speaking about burnout as something that happens to you all of a sudden, it is more accurately an insidious, progressive form of self-neglect. In its worst state, it represents a kind of slow deterioration that eventually rusts and corrodes the edges of your compassion and caring.

WINDOW INTO A CLASSROOM

Last year, Amanda was in the middle of her third year of teaching. If you had dropped into her fifth-grade classroom, you would not have guessed that she was still a relatively new teacher.

She did not struggle, as many rookie teachers do, to control disruptive students. She was not disturbed when the principal popped in unexpectedly to conduct an annual evaluation of her teaching. Her bulletin boards were filled with colorful illustrations; her walls were lined with examples of outstanding student work. Had you taken a quick look at her lesson plan book, you would have been impressed to find that she was not just slightly ahead in her planning—she had completed her lessons for the entire school year.

This window into Amanda's classroom one year ago might present the picture of a fulfilled teacher, that is, if you did not look very closely. The fact is, as Amanda later admitted, she was exhibiting the signs of a form of burnout that Gmelch (1983) describes as *rustout*.

Rustout is a type of burnout that afflicts teachers when they temporarily or permanently cease to be enthusiastic learners. The excitement of learning is what first attracted many teachers like Amanda to the classroom. Learning provides the joy, delight, and wonder that leaves little room for boredom or going-through-the-motions routines. Learning sustains interest, promotes risk taking, and rewards the teacher with the energy required to continue the hard work of exploring, searching, stretching, inventing, constructing, and so on.

If you had observed more carefully Amanda's classroom last year, you would have come to recognize the clear evidence of the onset of her professional rusting out. Look at those bulletin boards again. Sure, they are colorful, but they are also laminated to child-proof them and preserve them for next year's use. These flower-filled spring scenes decorate the room, but they do not invite her students to use them as tools for learning.

Check out her examples of high-quality student work that line the walls. The writing samples are error free, but bear a striking resemblance to one another. They show no evidence of the impishly delightful senses of humor of fifth-grade students. Not one piece of writing rings with the authentic voice of a vibrant child. The lesson plans, so dutifully prepared for the entire year, provide another piece of evidence of the rigid, risk-avoiding environment that paralyzes the learning of Amanda's students. She was no longer an effective model of learning. She was cruising the class on automatic pilot. Although she appeared to be efficiently moving her students from Grade 5 to Grade 6, the magic was gone. Amanda was an unknowing victim of rustout.

That was last year. This year, at the beginning of the second semester, Amanda's deadly routine was abruptly changed when she was requested to supervise a student teacher. Maryann came into Amanda's class in January, filled with a vision of limitless learning opportunities for her first class of real fifth-grade students.

She made the mistakes any beginning teacher would make and agonized over them, but learned to get back on track. She kept one step ahead of her students and frequently found ways of using their diversions as paths to unplanned but powerful learning.

For science, Maryann took her students out to an adjacent vacant lot, staked out a 4-by-6-foot plot for each student, and showed them how to observe and describe the conditions of the soil, weeds, and insects of their piece of ground. During the semester, the students inspected their piece of earth weekly, measuring the growth of plants, noting the effects of pollution, and sharing concern about people's insensitivity to the care of the earth.

Maryann's bulletin boards were interactive centers where students learned to create limericks, solve mathematical story problems, and fill out questionnaires about issues vital to fifth graders. She displayed many samples of her students' writing, most of them works in progress, such as the letters each was writing to a favorite author. There were no paint-by-numbers kinds of student work. Maryann had taken the time to discover the multiple abilities of all her students. Their artwork and poems, their recipes and story problems revealed the unique gifts of culturally diverse children.

Maryann revealed another admirable quality of a genuine teacher—she stayed consistently and consciously on the learning curve. She learned from those peers who were eager to share the wonder of their professional lives with her. She learned from sharing her highs and lows each evening with her husband. From her master teacher, Amanda, she learned how to implement the district curriculum, consult with parents, and organize students for tasks such as food collections, picture taking, and fire drills. Maryann consciously learned from her students, who eagerly shared their unique skills, hobbies, and experiences with her and with their classmates. Some of the students came from wealthy families; they shared experiences and artifacts collected on vacations to Washington, D.C., Paris, and New York City. Other students were the sons and daughters of migrant farm workers. They shared stories and mementos from their travels to the cotton fields of Texas, the vineyards of California, and the orchards of Oregon.

Most of all, however, Maryann learned from herself. She learned from trial and error. Her mistakes were not sources of shame; they were challenges to construct new learning approaches. She learned to trust her instincts about her students' growth. She learned about her own values and how to affirm them without unduly influencing the beliefs of her peers or her students. She learned her limits, but she also learned to constantly test these boundaries. She learned that neither she nor her students were perfect, but she recognized that they did not have to settle for mediocrity. She daily challenged herself and others to strive for excellence. Most of all, she learned that the major source of rewards for her hard work as a teacher came from belonging to a community of lifelong learners who genuinely care about each other.

Needless to say, Maryann's student teaching was highly successful. It provided her with the guided practice and feedback she needed to successfully launch her career in teaching. It also created a turning point in the career of her master teacher, Amanda, who was unconsciously in the grip of professional rustout. "I never expected that a student teacher would make learning fun for me again. I can't wait to get my students back and start over again."

Starting over again is what Amanda realized she must consciously do at the beginning of each school year to avoid the stultifying effects of rustout. The powerful daily demonstrations of genuine learning orchestrated by her enthusiastic student teacher had so transformed Amanda's students from reluctant participants to eager learners that Amanda was convinced that she had to change. Maryann's daily modeling of student-centered learning also gave Amanda the potent remedy she needed to master burnout and rustout and to transform her future classrooms into laboratories for student learning.

The paradigm shift Amanda made in her professional life from a teacher-centered to a student-centered philosophy also affected her at the core of her being. She initiated a program focused on attacking burnout and rustout in her personal life. Rustout, she realized, had also been eroding her marriage and her relationship with her two children. When her husband refused to seek counseling with her to put back the spark in their marriage, Amanda sought counseling for herself. This support helped her to improve her self-esteem and communications skills. Amanda also rewarded herself with a conscious program of personal growth experiences. A regular program of exercise combined with sensible eating helped her overcome years of "yo-yo" weight-loss/weight-gain cycles. She rediscovered the joy of reading. She attended concerts and public lectures. She found new delights in taking bit parts in community theater. Most of all,

Amanda's new perspective on life gave her a sense of personal and professional efficacy she had never experienced before. She was learning how to make a real difference in her own life and in the lives of her family, friends, and students.

SOURCES OF STRESS

We have described the processes of rustout and burnout as essentially resulting from excessive stress in the workplace, especially from the demands placed on teachers by others. The teaching profession is among the most stressful of all occupations because of the daily unrelenting pressures and fragmented demands from a number of sources—students, parents, and administrators as well as from the teachers themselves (Blase, 1991; Blase & Kirby, 1999). Linda Darling-Hammond tells us "High poverty schools suffer higher rates of attrition for many reasons" (Darling-Hammond, 2003, p. 8). Besides having lower salaries, teachers in these schools have "fewer resources, poorer working conditions, and the stress of working with many students and families who have a wide range of needs" (Darling-Hammond, 2003, p. 8).

In a study of why teachers burn out, Friesen, Prokop, and Sarros (1988) concluded that there are three main reasons. The first factor, emotional exhaustion, is the logical consequence of overextending yourself—emotionally and physically—trying to do too much or to keep up with a workload that is overwhelming. The second factor, depersonalization, describes what takes place when teachers develop negative attitudes toward others with whom they work. They become cynical, frustrated, and critical. The third factor, according to the researchers, is the lack of personal accomplishment. Burned-out teachers feel discouraged and disillusioned because they are not satisfying their own needs for challenges, recognition, and appreciation. They feel discouraged about themselves because their work does not provide them with sufficient feelings of fulfillment.

These three factors operating in teacher burnout are the same ones identified by Maslach and Jackson (1981) in an earlier report on occupational stress. Gold (1988) has further summarized the causes as belonging to two main sources: the teacher's personality characteristics and the conditions of the workplace. The following is a list of three types of teachers most likely to experience burnout:

1. Young and inexperienced people

2. Ambitious, driven people who had achievement-oriented parents

3. Loners who are unable to express feelings and have a propensity to be depressed

You can therefore appreciate that beginners are just as much at risk for burnout as are experienced teachers. That is one reason many new teachers quit their jobs within the first three years.

This is especially the case if they have certain personality characteristics that predispose them to greater risk of stress and burnout—if they are driven and ambitious, have perfectionist attitudes, are impatient and competitive, and do not feel in control of their emotions (see Farber & Wechler, 1991; Maslach & Leiter, 1997; Mills, Powell, & Pollack, 1992).

In addition to these internal factors that predispose certain people to rustout or burnout, there are also a number of external factors that are part of the teacher's role of answering to so many different people. For example, most schools are still hierarchically organized in such a way that they prevent teachers from collaborating together. Teachers spend most of the day in a room by themselves without any contact with other adults. Furthermore, a teacher's whole professional life is ruled by bells signaling that it is time to move on to another activity whether you are ready to do so or not. And, when teachers do get together for a meeting, they are short, maybe an hour, and focus primarily on announcements rather than interaction. One director of student teaching observed after supervising hundreds of beginning teachers, "How can we be reflective or work cooperatively with colleagues when our time is so filled by an imposed structure?"

In the Teacher Follow-up Survey data collected by the National Center for Education Statistics after the Schools and Staffing Survey (SASS) the main reasons new teachers give for leaving the profession besides low salaries are: "student discipline problems, lack of support from administration; poor student motivation, and lack of teacher influence over school-wide and classroom decision-making" (Ingersoll & Smith, 2003, p. 32).

We want you to understand clearly the real challenges you will face on a daily basis. Our intention is not to discourage or frighten you into switching to a different profession, especially when the need for teachers is so high; rather it is to equip you with the knowledge about what you will encounter so that (a) you will not be surprised, and (b) you will not be without resources and tools with which you can vigorously counteract negative effects.

So much of what determines how teachers will react to potentially stressful situations depends on the attitudes they have trained themselves to respond with. We therefore encourage you to treat each of these sources of stress as a challenge to be faced rather than a problem to be overcome. This attitude allows you to confront potentially difficult situations not as wars to be won (which will doom you to frustration and failure), but as obstacles to be negotiated. Nowhere will this approach be more helpful to you than when dealing with difficult and uncooperative children.

Difficult Students

"Teaching would be a great job . . . if only we didn't have to deal with students," one cynical practitioner was heard to say. Indeed, one of the most common complaints made by teachers around the world is about those children who misbehave and are uncooperative. As mentioned above, the literature on teacher burnout reveals that among the greatest stressors to teachers with five years or less experience is classroom discipline of disruptive, incorrigible students. These are the students, whether emotionally disturbed or simply ornery, whose primary mission in life it seems is to disrupt classroom proceedings and make the teacher's life as miserable as possible.

The comedian George Carlin, one of the most famous disruptive students of all time, freely admits he got most of his training as an entertainer while attending parochial schools. What better place, he reasoned, to hone one's skills of making people laugh than in a setting where they are under such strict prohibitions not to do so? Carlin therefore perfected his now-famous routines of disrupting the class and infuriating the teacher through an ingenious assortment of obscene sounds, noises, and miscellaneous tricks. His favorite was "the pigeon," because he could make the sound deep in his throat, swallowing obnoxiously but unobtrusively, all the while looking around with everyone else trying to identify the culprit.

Carlin and other class clowns just like him are repeatedly asked by exasperated teachers, "Why do you do this? Why must you behave so atrociously?" The obvious reply, of course, is, "Because it is fun." Think back to your school days: It was such delight to engage in forbidden activities, to break rules, to test yourself against authority figures, to make your friends laugh. During a time when you did not feel very much in control of your body or your life, when parents, teachers, and other grown-ups were always telling you what to do and how and when to do it, what exhilarating power you felt proving that you could get to one of them by making a teacher mad.

This is not all innocent fun. The class clown is more a source of minor annoyance (and sometimes even secret delight to the teacher with a sense of humor) than of serious stress and opposition. There are other children, however, whose disruptive behavior results not so much from harmless mischief as from some serious emotional disturbance. They are the children with major chips on their shoulders and axes to grind—especially with adults in positions of power over them. Many of them have been verbally and physically abused; others have been neglected or emotionally abandoned. Still others are just downright ornery: constitutionally obnoxious. They are hostile, seething with rage. They may be sociopathic, without conscience or moral responsibility. Others are just lost, aimless, nihilistically striking out at whoever is readily available. Many of them carry weapons and engage in fantasies of seeking violent revenge.

Regardless of the reasons why some children misbehave—whether they are crying out for help or just plain mean—they present a constant source of stress for teachers who must find ways to neutralize their inappropriate conduct (see Kosier, 1998; Kottler, 2002). Discipline problems are, after all, the number one complaint by teachers as to what they dislike most about this work.

Peek into one "classroom from hell" where the teacher is trying to get through a lesson:

Teacher: Frieda, would you please stop whispering to Sasha and pay attention.

Frieda: I wasn't whispering to Sasha; she was whispering to me.

Sasha: I was not!

Frieda: Yes, you were!

Teacher: That's enough! Both of you . . . Hey, over there—I asked you boys to put those pictures away. You can look at them after school.

A voice: Go to hell, teacher! You can sit on my pictures.

Teacher: Who said that? I want to know right now who said that! (Silence for the first time that hour)

Teacher: Now, where were we?

A voice: Sitting on Mike's pictures.

Teacher: Felipe, I heard that. Are you saying that Mike was the one who yelled that out?

Mike: It wasn't me. (Aside to Felipe): I'm going to kick your ass after school.

Teacher: Well, I don't think this is very funny. Sasha and Frieda, would you please stop whispering again?

Well, you get the picture. This is enough to create a major headache for almost any teacher. What is important at this point is not how you should handle discipline situations such as this, but that you recognize defiance and opposition by students are a normal part of a teacher's life. Even the most experienced classroom managers who follow the research-based strategies for effective classrooms face discipline problems. Day after day, mediating these petty skirmishes; breaking up fights and conflicts; and feeling compelled to threaten, cajole, sometimes even scream like a banshee take their toll on the most tranquil educator, especially if steps are not taken to bring the students (and yourself) under control.

In discipline situations, such as the one described earlier, we can identify the components of effective classroom management with student-teacher relationships as the foundation. Marzano (2003) offers the following research-based practices for teachers:

1. Establish and enforce rules and procedures for expected behavior. Rules and procedures need to be set at the beginning of the school year (or whenever a new teacher assumes responsibility of the classroom) in order to maintain an orderly and safe environment and promote smooth transitions between activities. Rules focus on interaction between,

and among, the teacher and students and respecting property. Procedures cover the beginning and end of day routines, handling materials, group work, and movement.

2. Carry out disciplinary action. This occurs in the form of commendations and rewards for positive behavior and negative consequences for inappropriate behavior. All of this occurs within the context of a relationship that is cooperative and respectful.

3. Maintain an appropriate mental set. Effective teachers have a high degree of "with-it-ness," that is, knowing what is going on the classroom at all times by constantly monitoring behavior to stop any inappropriate behavior when it begins and before it escalates to a point where it disrupts the class.

4. Demonstrate "emotional objectivity." The best teachers implement their discipline policies calmly, without becoming upset or taking things personally. They focus on the situation and on the student behavior not the student as a bad or problematic person.

5. Become aware of the different needs of students. As they respond to different academic needs, so, too, do teachers respond to inappropriate behavior in varying ways using a variety of strategies.

Irate Parents

Second on the list of gripes among veteran teachers, after problem students, is difficult parents. What makes some parent conferences such dreaded events in the life of a teacher is the persistent, irrational, and misguided belief on the part of some people that their children are misunderstood, unappreciated, and unfairly treated. If only the teacher were more competent/intelligent/patient/ skilled/ experienced (choose one), then their child would not be having these problems. For those parents who do not want to accept responsibility for their children's academic or behavior problems, the easiest thing to do is to blame the teacher.

In its most civilized form, the parent hassle involves subjecting the teacher to subtle put-downs and insinuations of neglect or incompetence: "I suppose you are doing your best, given what you have to work with," or, "My son never had these problems before he entered your class. I guess it must be a coincidence, huh?"

Some parents become belligerent, make threats, even act dramatically hostile in their accusations: "My daughter says you don't like her. That's why she doesn't do her homework or study for your dumb tests. I'm going to the principal to have you fired!" When the situation becomes heated or out of control, teachers need to disengage, end the conference, and reschedule it for a later date after all parties have calmed down. Teachers should remove themselves from conflicts that can, in rare situations, become abusive. When the conference reconvenes, a counselor or administrator should be present.

Parents are not our enemies. Many have had negative school experiences of their own in the past. Others are facing a host of problems in their personal and professional lives, and coming to school to see a teacher during their work day perhaps adds to the inconveniences and embarrassments of their lives. As you get to know them, you will learn about their backgrounds. Many parents are uncomfortable in schools and try to cover it up with loud talk. Although these experiences are frustrating and disappointing, many schools and districts are working to develop programs to improve relationships with parents.

In most cases, parents are our greatest allies whose support and encouragement make our jobs so much easier. During consultations, most parents only want to know what they can do to help their children and us in the educational process. They value our efforts and appreciate our dedication. Most of the time, if a parent does become unreasonable or disrespectful, an apology will quickly follow with the realization and acknowledgment, "I know you are doing the best you can. It's just that we have done all we can think of to try and motivate our daughter, and nothing seems to work. Now, we are expecting you to fix it all in a matter of months. You tell us what we can do to help."

All parents have dreams of their child becoming a neurosurgeon, trial attorney, professional athlete, corporate president, or U.S. senator. When evidence in the form of underachievement begins to show up, the parents' expectations are cracked, if not shattered. Parents want their children to have more than they had, to be more than they have been. You have felt these same pressures from your own parents throughout your life. Your disappointments become their failures. Your setbacks become their inadequacies. Because school performance is the primary measurement of childhood achievement in our society, each report card and parent-teacher conference is fraught with anxiety—"Is this the time when I will face the fact that my child is a loser?"

Needless to say, conferences with parents can easily become emotionally charged. There is a tremendous amount at stake. Things must be handled very carefully and diplomatically by the teacher, creating a tremendous amount of strain and stress. Once a teacher has been beaten up verbally by an irate parent, all future conferences may be dreaded as potentially explosive. This pressure is heaped on top of other kinds of interpersonal difficulties that are often part of the political and social organizations called schools.

Collegial Backbiting

It is ironic that the teacher must contend with not only pressures from without—difficult students and parents, a public with little regard or respect for the profession—but also interpersonal strains from within the school. Some teachers report that they encounter little difficulty from students or their parents; the problems come from their own colleagues. One veteran teacher with 15 years of experience describes this situation:

> I love teaching. When I am in the classroom, the whole world stops for me. I don't have a problem in the world. Most of the kids are great to work with, and even the ones who are feisty eventually come around with a little patience, support, and firm limits. I rarely have problems with parents, either. They just like to be treated as partners and want a chance to blow off a little steam.
>
> If I could just be left alone with my kids, everything would be wonderful. All of my stress comes from dealing with my colleagues, so I try to stay away from them. There are only a few people I will eat lunch with because those are the ones who aren't so threatened by new ideas and who genuinely like kids. All that the other teachers do is talk about one another behind each other's backs and complain all the time. They complain about playground duty. They complain about the custodians. They complain about the heating, the parking, the administration, the union, their salaries. Most of all, however, they complain about the kids. I just try to stay out of their way and do my job.

Misery loves company, and in some schools, it abounds in the teacher's lounge as this teacher describes. Those who do not support "the cause" and do not speak in conformity with the others will feel pressure from those who do.

A school is no different from any other human organization. We have a collection of well-educated, highly experienced people who are experts at imparting knowledge and skills to others. They are used to talking and having others pay close attention, even take notes on what they are saying. All of these professionals have healthy egos and strong opinions and want to be respected by their peers. What we have, then, is an enriched but enmeshed school environment. Coalitions and political factions are inevitable within departments and within the local teacher association. Administrators and school board members are often viewed with suspicion and distrust. All too frequently, the principals are seen less as benevolent supervisors than as tyrants, authorities who get in the way of teachers doing their jobs with various mandates of their own or from the district office.

In spite of what the disillusioned teacher said earlier in this section, teaching is the kind of job in which you need collegial support to survive, much less to flourish. It is imperative that you feel that you belong to a group of peers who share your values and interests and, most of all, whom you can trust. Stress effects from other sources are magnified when your collegial relationships are less than supportive.

STRESS MANAGEMENT STRATEGIES

Each of the sources of stress previously mentioned, although experienced by many educators, need not inevitably tear you down. You can prepare yourself with a number of strategies, such as those described next, that will serve you well in your efforts to stay calm and comfortable, even in the face of very difficult circumstances.

Building a Support System

Probably the single most important thing that you can do to keep yourself energized and to prevent the rustout that stems from the sources of stress just mentioned is to create a support system that offers you nurturance, compassion, understanding, and direction when it is needed. Family and friends are, of course, important to help you diversify your relationships and provide support and acceptance. A surrogate family at work is just as important, made up of those colleagues whom you most trust. Early in your career, these colleagues will be important in showing you the routines of your school and in sharing with you all the do's and don'ts expected by the principal, the other faculty members, and the parents at your school. Some teachers prefer to find colleagues to talk to from outside of their school and so make a special effort to attend as many inservice programs as possible. It does not make much difference how you arrange your collegial support, as long as you do something constructive, such as developing a place in which you feel safe and accepted and understood.

For those teachers who enjoy or require even more intense and stimulating supportive experiences, there is also the option of joining a counseling or therapy group. This is not necessarily done because teachers perceive they have emotional problems; rather they wish to find an environment that will help them to grow. In one such group designed specifically for teachers, a number of issues arose that have universal appeal:

"Is what I'm doing with my life really all that worthwhile?"

"How can I change the routines of my life so that they don't seem so repetitive and boring?"

"Now that I'm settled into a career and a lifestyle, is this all there is?"

"I am so good at being loving at work with the children. How come I have so much trouble finding a good relationship outside of work?"

"What can I do to take care of the problem I am having with my spouse? Nothing I've tried so far seems to work."

These and similar personal and professional questions are considered during a teacher's normal reflective time. Regardless of the teacher's discipline, specialty, or institutional level, most teachers tend to be reflective and inquiring. We live a lifestyle that encourages us to consider difficult questions, to read and study, to make sense of the world, and to help others to do the same. This is sometimes lonely, very painful work. You will need lots of help along the way.

Learning to Relax

Relaxation involves letting go of all troubles and distractions. It means releasing all stress and strains in your life. Most of all, relaxation is a form of "time out," in which your body and mind are permitted to recuperate and rejuvenate themselves, especially after intense periods of work.

People relax in an endless number of ways—through meditation, listening to music, watching television, driving in the car, walking, hiking, exercising, daydreaming, watching movies, soaking in a bath, playing with a computer, watching birds, or working on a hobby. The point is that these activities are not merely for entertainment, diversion, and leisure; they are necessary for you to function productively in other areas of your life.

Due to the everyday strains that teachers must face, it is absolutely imperative that ways be found to metabolize and dissipate the stress. If not, your rustout process will accelerate quickly or, perhaps even worse, you will resort to less healthy ways to deal with things. Alcohol and other substance abuse, overeating, and other self-destructive habits are often the result of people's attempts to medicate themselves for the stress they feel in their lives. The time to begin lifelong relaxation patterns is right now. If you wait until you feel that you are in over your head, more drastic solutions will be needed to pull yourself out.

Relaxation really means taking time out for yourself. It involves doing something for a period of time that is just for you. You are able, at least temporarily, to put all other aspects of your life aside while you concentrate on a single activity that makes you feel good. Right this moment, think about the stress you feel in your life, the pressures you carry around. There are people who have certain expectations for you, expectations you can never (or choose not to) live up to. There are obligations, tasks, responsibilities, burdens that must be met. There are relationships in your life that are conflicted or unfulfilled. There may be financial or time pressures that you are living with.

Just imagine adding to all the existing strains in your life the additional challenge of an everyday teaching job. Furthermore, picture one particular class you have, with more than its fair share of problem kids who are belligerent and unresponsive to all your efforts. What will you do to keep yourself calm in the face of defiance and opposition? How will you maintain your composure when the pressures pile on top of you?

In addition to any leisure pursuits or recreational activities you might pursue to help yourself relax, there are also strategies that are helpful during stressful situations. Most of these involve talking to yourself in such a way that you feel in control, a methodology that is a direct application of the cognitive interventions we discussed in the previous chapter on helping skills.

The following reminders are often helpful for teachers to repeat to themselves during the inner dialogue that takes place during stressful situations:

- They aren't doing this to me; they are doing it to themselves.
- What can I do differently?
- This isn't personal.
- Where is the humor in this situation?
- It could be worse.
- In what ways am I exaggerating or distorting things?
- What in me is getting in the way of responding more empathically?

When all else fails, one well-tried technique involves simply taking a deep breath, letting the oxygen cleanse you, and focusing all your attention, for even a few seconds, on centering yourself (you might try this right now, for practice). You may be surprised at what a difference brief relaxation exercises such as this can make in helping you retain your composure and serenity.

A Healthy Lifestyle

The way in which you structure your life will determine, to a great extent, how well you will cope with unexpected bumps along the road. This includes such things as sleeping patterns, eating habits, ingestion of alcohol, even the pace at which you conduct your daily affairs. A teacher's lifestyle is an unusual one, structured as it is with working hours and vacations that are distinctly different from those of the business world. In fact, many professionals readily admit that the reason they chose teaching in the first place is that they liked the idea of getting home in the afternoon each day and having summers off. Yet, in spite of these windows of opportunity, this time off, which is specifically designed to encourage teachers to rejuvenate themselves, is often filled with additional burdens. Some teachers even find other jobs they can work during summers to supplement their incomes. The price they pay, of course, is sacrificing the qualitative longevity of their careers in exchange for meeting perceived economic needs.

One teacher explains, "Look, you think I like painting houses after school and during the summer? I don't do this because it's fun or I'm greedy or anything; my family needs this money to survive." When queried further as to what the extra money is used for, it becomes evident that its primary purpose is to provide for added luxuries—a boat, a sports car, a larger house that would be otherwise unaffordable. This teacher is willing to give up free time to make his family more comfortable. Although this motive is laudable, when fall rolls around and the new school year is about to begin, he is already exhausted, whereas many of his colleagues return refreshed and eager.

A teacher with a lifestyle radically different from the previous one explains his philosophy:

> Sure, we would have more money, more things, if I supplemented our income with a part-time job. There are many things I wish I could afford. But I'm not willing to give up my precious time once I'm out of school. Since I work during prep periods during the school days, when the bell rings, I feel just like the kids: free for the afternoon and evenings. I like to spend this time with my family or puttering around the house. Because I get home before my wife, I'm in charge of cooking dinner, which I really enjoy. I finish up any grading or planning I might need to do after dinner. By the time school starts the next morning, I feel really rested.
>
> Summers are even more wonderful for me. I look at this time as two and a half months of uninterrupted indulgence, in that I can do whatever I want. I like to read novels, fix things around the house, go for long walks, sleep late. And then there is the travel . . . Wow! I usually try to take a month just for myself—seeing some part of the country or the world. Then, we

usually take a lengthy family trip somewhere. Last summer, we spent a month camping and hiking in British Columbia.

By the time school begins, I am usually restless and more than ready to get started. Ten weeks is a long time to be off with no structure. It really helps me to appreciate the daily routines of the school year.

It is important to take a step back from all the demands on your time to examine your values and your goals. Determine what is important to you, reasonable expectations, and time lines. For example, if you are interested in a M.A. degree, explore all the various public, private, traditional, and online programs available. Identify short-term, school-related goals (improving technology skills or revising a unit) and personal goals (weeding your lawn, going to the movies or a concert), as well as long-term, school-related goals (becoming a school counselor or a principal) and personal goals, (learning to play the piano or redecorating your house). The secret is to set your goals, prioritize the items on your "things to do" list, identify the time and resources you need for each item and plan a calendar.

One of my (E. K.) early mentors asked me every Friday what I was going to do for fun every weekend. Although as a first-year teacher, I sometimes did work through the weekend during the first month of school, this question helped me recognize that I needed to balance my activities. I could see I would burn out if I didn't make time for family and friends and some time just for myself, which for me was some quiet, relaxing reading time or going to the movies. I began planning ahead and as time went on, I would wait for her question with a ready answer.

At the same time, I had to explain to my parents and new boyfriend that while my work day officially ended at 3:45 p.m., I still needed time at home in the evening and sometimes on the weekend to prepare for the next day. Plus, one night a week I was taking a graduate course and had to study for that class as well. I separated myself from these activities when I was with them and let them know how much I appreciated their support. There were some times when I didn't want to be around anybody. I needed my "alone" time.

There are few other occupations that offer such a flexible lifestyle and so many opportunities for using your free time in fulfilling ways. But there is the danger of squandering this time, filling it with more burdens and obligations. There are so many opportunities at schools to be involved from committees to school clubs, to afterschool and evening programs for children and adults. The requests may seem endless. You can't do it all effectively all of the time. Guard your schedule. It is up to you to structure your own life, plan your own time, teach others how to treat you, if you wish to reap the benefits of the teacher's lifestyle.

Training and Growth

The best way to deal with burnout and rustout is to avoid it in the first place. Do not let yourself ever get to the point where your discouragement becomes intractable. Kaikai and Kaikai (1990) suggest, for example, that the best way teachers can stay fresh and energized is to have the courage and determination to keep making changes in what they do and how they do it. This includes, but is not limited to, the following list:

- Request different teaching assignments every few years, with a different grade level or specialty area.
- Take a sabbatical to study and update your areas of expertise.
- Do a faculty exchange with a teacher from another country.
- Invite other professionals and resource people into your classroom to liven things up.
- Arrange team-teaching assignments with another staff member or university faculty member.
- Supervise a student teacher.
- Go back to school.
- Organize more field trips and out-of-class activities.
- Start a research project for publication or to present at a conference.
- Apply for grants to study abroad.
- Integrate cutting-edge technology into your methods.

Teachers sometimes dislike "command performances," in which they are required to attend professional development activities. Why not gather together a like-minded group of colleagues and start your own training and growth activities? You could start by sharing the individual expertise you already own. One colleague might share how she uses a spreadsheet to keep track of grades; another might share how he structures parent conferences to promote student learning at home; another describes use of a web page and distance learning methods. Perhaps you could occasionally invite an expert in to share a particular skill or strategy at a brown-bag lunch break. Such a grassroots professional development movement might even grow to the point where it aids in establishing a school culture where students, parents, teachers, administrators, and community members grow and learn together.

Keeping a Journal

A number of authors recommend that persons in the helping professions allocate a portion of time each week for reflective thought. This is a time for you to consider where you have been, where you are now, and where you are headed in the future. It is a time for questioning the meaning of your actions and, ultimately, the overriding purpose of your life.

Two famous contemporary teachers—John Holt, author of *How Children Learn* (1968) and *How Children Fail* (1964), and Pat Conroy, author of a multitude of novels, including *The River Is Wide, The Lords of Discipline, The Great Santini,* and *The Prince of Tides*—found their journals to be instrumental in helping them to release tension as well as unleash their creative powers. Journal writing has a number of other important values for teachers:

- A record of your thoughts, feelings, dreams, fears, failures, and accomplishments allows you to trace recurring patterns of your life, identifying prevalent themes, unresolved issues, and unfinished business.
- A journal becomes a place where you can dump all your daily frustrations and joys, without fear of judgment or criticism. It is an utterly safe place to store your most private thoughts and feelings.
- It is a place where you can note teaching strategies and discipline methods that work, as well as those that do not. You can even begin this process right now, beginning a personal resource book of ideas you want to remember and have access to at a future time. Some teachers like to save favorite quotes they have read. Others like to catalog all the funny things that children say and do.

- A journal is a place for you to set goals for yourself. Where would you like to be and what do you want to be doing one, five, ten years from now? Commit yourself in writing, and let that act as an impetus to help push you forward toward what you have declared is most important.
- You can experiment with new ways of thinking, feeling, and behaving in your journal. You can try out new roles, play with novel ideas, pretend to make certain changes in your life as a dress rehearsal before taking action.

Most of all, a journal is a place where you can talk to yourself. It helps you develop self-discipline and greater precision and sensitivity in your communication. In this process of systematic self-reflection, you become more insightful about your own inner world and thus better attuned to your desires and needs. You are able to work through internal conflicts, solve personal problems, remember significant events that take place, and be more like the person that you want to be. "It is in the process of clarification that journaling, or any activity of solitary reflection, allows you to regain a sense of meaning to your life" (Kottler, 1990, p. 123).

Maintaining Momentum

By the time burnout sets in, it is often too late to recover sufficiently to reclaim your initial enthusiasm. The time to start is *before* you begin to feel burned out. In Table 7.1, we summarize a few of the things you can do in this regard.

As Williams (2003) describes, the teaching profession allows individuals a high level of autonomy and creativity in their work with rewards that are meaningful. Teachers know they make a difference in the lives of their students. Their teaching continues to evolve as they continue to learn from their experiences and share their expertise with others. Their needs for stimulation, creativity, and belonging are met by collaborating with others and supporting their colleagues and their needs.

Finding meaning to your work, even with the aggravation and stress you will occasionally be subjected to, is the key to preventing burnout and to keeping rustout at bay. Such reflective activities as writing in a journal help you to remain clear and vital, as well as intensely aware of what is going on inside you and around you.

Table 7.1   Teacher Strategies That Maintain Momentum

- Study teachers who are successful.
- Be selective about who you hang out with.
- Have realistic expectations for what can be done.
- Push yourself to take risks and try new things.
- Take victories where you can get them.
- Find the best in people.
- Set limits.
- Nurture and nourish yourself throughout the day.
- Remember that it's relationships, not content, that matter most.
- Keep a sense of humor.
- Diversify interests and commitments.
- Don't work excessively at home.
- Stop caring about things you can't do anything about.
- Stop whining and complaining.
- See yourself through students' eyes.
- Make it a priority to keep learning fun.

Being reflective is, in fact, the single most important commitment that teachers can make to keep themselves invigorated about their work.

SUGGESTED ACTIVITIES

1. Interview experienced teachers regarding their first year of teaching to find out how and why they were able to be successful their first year and how they have maintained their momentum.

2. Begin a journal in which you set aside time weekly for reflective thought on where you are now and where you are headed.

3. Observe how classroom teachers maintain classroom management. Watch how they supervise students when working one-on-one with a student, with small groups of students, and with the whole class. Determine what rules are in effect, what procedures have been established, and how the discipline policy is implemented.

4. Evaluate your life in relation to the responsibilities and commitments you have. How does or will teaching make an impact on your family and friends?

5. Consider the strategies in Table 7.1, and choose three to begin to emphasize in your life.

CHAPTER EIGHT

On Being Reflective

Do you save aluminum cans? Perhaps you are one of the many North Americans who carefully spend time sifting their garbage to help save the dwindling resources of our world. Although conservation of our natural resources is important, there is another resource valuable to our personal and professional lives that teachers seldom take care of—spending time daily sifting through our minds and hearts, reflecting on how we can become more interesting and resourceful. Think of all the valuable ideas, hunches, insights, and feelings you will trash if you fail to become a reflective person and professional.

On the path to becoming a teacher, there are many skills to acquire and much professional knowledge to accumulate before you are finally entrusted with your own students. During the past two decades, this focus on the acquisition of technical knowledge and skills in teacher preparation programs has emphasized a prescriptive view of teaching, one that follows rules and procedures by formula. During this same period of time, many educational publishing companies developed so-called teacher-proof textbooks and instructional programs, which provide elaborate guidelines and scripts for use in classrooms by prescriptive teachers. Teachers would not have to think, just follow the instructions provided.

Early in the 1980s, a reaction to this notion of teacher-as-classroom-technician prompted a return to a tradition that values the reflective teacher. At the present time, many teacher education programs are rushing to infuse reflection into their courses and field experiences. This practice is reinforced by a strong emphasis on the importance of reflective teaching in the professional literature (Brandt, 1986; Eby, Herrell, & Hicks, 2001; Ghaye & Ghaye, 1998; Goethals, Howard, & Sanders, 2003; Guskey, 2000; Hole & McEntee, 1999; Kauchak & Eggen, 2005; Schon, 1987; Smyth, 1989).

We believe that reflection is a critical dimension of what it means to be an effective teacher. Unfortunately, this rapid swing toward urging teachers to be reflective appears to be based on the assumption that it is a simple task that is easily accomplished. The fact is that reflection is an extremely complex and demanding process that requires a lifetime of dedication.

On Being a Reflective Person

Although we could debate for some time whether reflective people are born or made—in other words, whether some people are naturally inclined to be contemplative or people learn to be that way, we take the position that anyone, whether a teacher or a student, can become more reflective if that person decides that this is an important goal and life priority. The first question to consider is whether being reflective is a good thing, a desirable outcome for people in general and for teachers in particular.

Being reflective essentially means being an independent thinker. It means knowing how to reason, to think for yourself, to combine intuition and logic in the process of solving problems. It means being introspective about phenomena that take place both within your internal world and in the world around you. This task, we believe, is among the most important missions of the teacher, for teaching involves so much more than presenting information, applying technical skills, or managing a group of children. It is a process by which people are taught to evaluate constructively.

Assuming that you believe that among the best things that you can accomplish in your work is to help children become more reflective themselves, more like fearless truth seekers, constructive risk takers, and inquiring thinkers, then the best way (and certainly the most authentic and congruent means) to accomplish this goal is by modeling the values you consider to be most sacred.

Carnie, for example, is sometimes criticized by her colleagues and department head because she strays from sanctioned objectives. Her job is to teach art appreciation, and her mandate is to encourage children to experiment with a number of artistic media. The problem, however, at least as it is labeled by her peers, is that she does not teach what she is supposed to teach. Any given class may find her wandering off course, provoking a discussion in the class about sexual and racial discrimination as they are manifested in art objects, or the impact of what is considered to be politically correct on artworks that have been commissioned throughout history.

Although Carnie sees herself as an art teacher, she considers herself to be, more than anything else, a stimulator of education that transcends disciplines. She wants her students to learn to love art; to value their own creative powers; and to understand that aesthetic efforts cannot be separated from political, historical, sociological, psychological, and literary movements of the time.

Carnie is a reflective professional because she considers that to be such an important priority for her own life. Although some of her colleagues may view her as "scattered," because she covers such vast territory in her interests, her students are captivated by her voracious appetite for knowledge and her intense desire to make sense of the world. They, too, have learned to become more reflective about the meaning of art in their lives and its place in the world of politics and commerce. Many of her students, even the very young ones, tend to begin their contributions in class with the preface, "I have been thinking about something that was said last time."

Children learn to be reflective when they can see for themselves that this is a valuable way to be. Even if it will not directly make them more money, win friends, and influence people, they will learn to find more peace within themselves and will develop more wisdom about the way the world works.

What It Means to Be Reflective

It should now be clear that becoming more reflective as a teacher depends very much on how you define yourself as a person. To attain this honorable self-concept, the following tasks are helpful:

Asking Why. The reflective person is inquisitive. This trait can sometimes be irritating to others who resent the determination on the part of an individual who constantly questions the status quo: "Why does it have to be done this way? Why can't things be done differently?" Of course, the reflective person also tends to consider most vehemently those questions that are least likely to lead to single, right answers: "What is the meaning of life? What is my mission here on earth? Why do people have to die? What happens after death?"

Finding Patterns. Being reflective means investing time and energy into trying to synthesize experiences, integrate knowledge, and bring together discrepant variables. It means being unrestricted by disciplines in the search for truth. The reflective person is constantly searching for the underlying reasons behind behavior and structures behind reality: "What makes people act the way they do? How do children learn and grow? What is the meaning of the collective silence in this classroom?"

The reflective person is intensely motivated to answer these and many other questions in the search for patterns of behavior and structures of the universe. In the truest sense of what it means to be a scholar, a renaissance individual, the reflective person attempts to advance the state of knowledge by formulating innovative conceptions about what has been observed.

Both of the first two mental exercises (asking why and finding patterns) operative in the reflective person are found in Carnie. She listens to a talk by a well-known author about the disappointments in his life. She reads a biography of Van Gogh and notes the different ways that he struggled with failure in his life. She considers her own life and the ways in which she has fought for acceptance, first from her parents, then from her colleagues.

Suddenly, a light bulb clicks on. An idea begins to take shape about the relationship between being disappointed and holding certain expectations for oneself and others. She begins to delve into the literature in psychology but finds little on the subject. She starts reading novelists who deal with themes of failure—Dostoyevsky, Camus, Conrad, Plath. She reads biographies of famous people who struggle with disappointment—Galileo, Columbus, Freud, Dickens. Finally, her idea begins to take a more definitive shape, which she is able to articulate in a unifying hypothesis: There is a relationship between the amount of time someone spends anticipating a particular event and the subsequent disappointment the person feels if things do not work out as expected.

It is not this particular idea, its validity or merits, that is important. Rather, it is the *way* in which Carnie's mind works. She is constantly searching for answers, trying to understand complex issues by tying together contributions from diverse sources. Carnie is an art teacher, but she is so much more.

Reading Voraciously. As is evident from the previous example, Carnie studies widely outside her own field. The reflective person, in order to make sense of things, must know about many different areas. It is not enough to be conversant in your discipline and professional identity; to be reflective you must also be knowledgeable about world events, contemporary and historical societal trends, political and economic events, the arts, humanities, and literature and even current films, television and radio shows, plays, fiction, and popular Web sites. In short, reflective people have taken the time to educate themselves about many different aspects of human existence.

Taking Time for Contemplation. Solitude is a necessity for the reflective person. It is absolutely crucial to have structured time alone to recover from the demands placed on you by others, to consider where you are headed in your life, simply to make time for you to be able to reach deep inside yourself to find out what you think and feel about what is taking place around you. The reflective person structures private time as part of daily life, no matter what family or professional demands exist. Without the time and the opportunity to be reflective, even with all the talent and the best intentions, serious contemplation cannot take place.

Examining Your Own Behavior. Reflective people are diligent students not only of world events and human behavior but also of their own actions. What good are wisdom and knowledge if you cannot apply them to your own life? Being reflective means considering the impact of your own behavior on others and accepting responsibility for the consequences of your actions. It means examining honestly what you are doing in your life and what effects (both positive and negative) you are having on others.

Confronting Excuses. Consistent with accepting responsibility for your actions is the belief that, with few exceptions, you are in charge of your own life. If things are not going the way you would like them to, rather than blaming others or making excuses, the reflective person prefers to take possession of the problem. Although giving up external reasons why things are not going according to plan is uncomfortable, as a reflective person, this also gives you a sense of personal power, of being in control of your own destiny.

Jose, an eighth-grade social studies teacher, is, at first, quite upset about the average ratings he received from his principal for classroom management. His first instinct is to make a number of excuses and to externalize the problem: "This isn't fair. The principal didn't take into consideration the larger class size she gave me this year. Besides, it's not my fault that some of my students can't keep on task for very long. Why does she seem to give me all the hyperactive kids?"

Whether these excuses are legitimate or not is beside the point (the brighter you are, the better excuses you will come up with for things not going your way). Jose decided that whether his principal evaluated him fairly or not, the bottom line was (a) he did not like feeling upset about something he could not change, and (b) he wanted to improve his classroom management skills for his own professional growth. Upon reflection, Jose much prefers the idea that he is the one who messed up; that way, the power is within him to do something to change it. Rather than blaming the principal, or himself, Jose decided to focus some of his attention on becoming more knowledgeable and proficient in motivating student involvement in learning social studies.

Defining Your Professional Mission. Being reflective means infusing your personal curiosity and truth-seeking values into your professional identity. To be a truly reflective person, you have to find a way to integrate the elements previously discussed into your style of teaching.

ON BECOMING A REFLECTIVE PROFESSIONAL

Personal reflection is a way of life, not just an interesting intellectual exercise. When you begin to acquire and value the habits of personal reflection, your professional life will be enriched. In this section, we focus our attention on creating an image of ourselves as reflective teachers. To create this image, we must first expand our understanding of what being a reflective teacher involves and why it is so important. Supported by this understanding, you can begin to prepare yourself to grow into the image of the reflective teacher you wish to become. We illustrate this process through the stories of two dedicated teachers at different stages of their career.

Terry: "It's Not the Way I Thought It Would Be."

My name is Terry. I have wanted to be a teacher for as long as I can remember. As a child, I used to play pretend games with my younger brothers and sisters; I was always the teacher, and they were my students.

So, it was natural for me to identify education as a major at the beginning of my college experience. I was so fortified by my experiences as a student tutor and inspired by outstanding models of excellent elementary teachers that I was even prepared to weather the criticisms of my college classmates about entering a low-paying, low-esteemed profession. I was also determined to endure what my classmates called "the frivolity of education classes," in order to get my teaching certificate. I had been ready for a long time to teach my own class of first-grade students.

I paid special attention to my methods classes and tried to acquire as much knowledge and as many teaching strategies as I could. I felt confident that because I really cared about students, I could reach them, especially if I had good command of teaching methods.

After I graduated, I was employed to teach fourth graders in an urban school district. Although I was disappointed in not receiving a first-grade assignment, I was happy that I got a job. Because I cared about kids of all ages, I thought I could be an effective fourth-grade teacher.

Something, however, was different; something was missing. My principal gave me a great evaluation for my classroom management abilities. The years of working with children in church activities and as a tutor had prepared me to be a good disciplinarian, and that was what he appeared to be mainly concerned about. However, a small segment of my students did not respond to me. I really cared about them. I tried everything I could think of to win them over, but they didn't seem to care. Most of these students were boys with short attention spans, hyperactivity, lack of motivation, low ability levels. You name it, they had it.

I was finally convinced that I couldn't do anything to help them with their problems. After all, I had to help 17 other students who really cared about learning. Some of my fellow teachers experienced similar resistance from some of their students. We used to trade war stories in the faculty lounge: "These kids just don't care. They watch too much television. They don't come to school ready to learn." Consequently, when we felt we could not do any more for these students, we referred them for a special education evaluation.

Don't get me wrong—while they were in my class I still cared for them. I did not put any pressure on them to learn. Many of them were minority students, and I was especially nice to them. While my academic students were working on story problems in math that required higher-level thinking skills, I let my nonacademic students work in the back of the room practicing arithmetic and then doing whatever they wanted, as long as they kept quiet. Some drew pictures of spaceships in combat with alien invaders. Others put their own words to rap songs. Silly things like that. I really didn't care what they did, as long as they did it without disturbing others. Some of the teachers in my school let their nonacademics take naps at their desks; I never let them do that.

Katherine: "I Don't Have Any Magic."

I'm Katherine. I have been an elementary teacher for 23 years. Twenty-three years is a long time, but I've enjoyed every minute of it. Well . . . most of them.

I've been encouraged to go into school administration, but I really am a teacher. I like working with students. I believe teaching begins and ends with students. I am truly proud of all my present and former students. They send me Christmas cards and invitations to their weddings years after they were students in my first-grade classroom.

My principal tells people that I was born with the ability to motivate students. He embarrasses me when he calls me a "classroom wizard" who casts the spell of lifelong learning on students. This makes some of my colleagues joke that I use some incantation or magic wand to motivate students to become eager about learning.

I don't have any magic. Furthermore, I really don't believe that I can motivate my students to learn. I do believe now, after thinking about it for many years, that motivation must come from inside my students. If I have a secret, it is that I talk frequently to each of my students. I get to know all about them, their hopes, their fears, what they dream about, what kinds of pain they have known. I try to find the gifts in all my students; I try to build on their strengths. Knowing as much as I can about them and how *they* view their world helps me to think of ways to tap into their inner motivation.

I consciously try to avoid naming and listing their limitations. When I discover their strengths, I search for significant learning experiences with which I can help them to build on their strengths. I try to structure my classroom space to encourage their active involvement in real learning. When they are really involved, I can become invisible and let them direct their own powerful learning. Most of the time, my students take responsibility for their learning; this success builds their self-esteem.

I also believe that I must establish a context for learning in which my students are encouraged to mutually esteem one another. I give them regular opportunities to share their lives and their interests with one another. What keeps me coming back to my classroom year after year, in addition to the warm vibrations I get from my students, are the many new things I learn and try. My principal calls me an "omnivore," because he says I attend every workshop, seminar, and professional conference I can. These professional activities give me a great deal of food for thought about being a better teacher, about being a better learner. I believe my enthusiasm for learning gives me a lot of material for teaching. I know it gives me real credibility with my students. They know I am a lifelong learner because they see I'm eager to learn outside of class and inside of class as well. Also, let me say this, because it's true: I have learned so much from my students that has really enriched my life.

Reflections on the Stories

Both of these teachers were highly successful in their undergraduate teacher education courses. They both got excellent letters of recommendation from their cooperating teachers, university supervisors, and principals. In some ways, they can both be considered effective teachers. They know their children very well and care very much about them. They use a variety of teaching strategies and have good classroom management. They even use reflection as a source for improving their teaching. With all these crucial features in common, what are their essential differences?

Of course, there are many differences in the levels of experience, professional attitudes, and personal beliefs. Both Terry and Katherine spent a considerable amount of time each day thinking carefully about the many decisions they had to make about learning experiences, instructional materials, classroom arrangements, and methods of instruction.

They were very different in their practice of "critical reflection." Critical reflection, as you will recall, is the other important dimension of what teachers must do when they think about their professional work. It is the kind of reflection that helps teachers understand and appreciate the moral, spiritual, aesthetic, and cultural dimensions of a teacher's responsibilities.

Review Terry's story, and you will see that she lacked essential understanding and appreciation. Although she told us over and over about the importance she placed on caring, she did place limits on her caring. Only those students she was able to reach without a struggle were the recipients of her caring. She gave up on those students who lacked motivation, students she labeled as mostly boys with short attention spans, hyperactivity, lack of motivation, and low ability levels. She did not reflect critically on her moral responsibility to become culturally sensitive to the needs of her minority students. Finally, she did not critically reflect on the aesthetic qualities of what these so-called nonacademic students accomplished. If she had carefully reflected on their drawings of spaceships in combat with alien invaders and their rap lyrics, she might have found a key to the motivation of real and durable learning experiences for these students. Unfortunately, Terry did what many other well-intentioned but nonreflective teachers do: She lowered her standards for these students and referred them to specialists.

Katherine, on the other hand, did not give up on any of her students. She considered, in a critical way, the level of development, the hopes, fears, aspirations, pains, and strengths of each of her students. She believed that it is her moral responsibility to structure her classroom and learning experiences to build on the strengths of each of her students. She consciously helped each one of her students to find the patterns of academic success they needed to build a solid foundation for their own self-esteem. She also encouraged her students to support one another through a celebration of their individual and collective accomplishments.

Katherine also was aesthetically sensitive to the importance of continuing the wonder of learning new things. She learned many things from her students; she learned many things from her colleagues and the many workshops she attended. Katherine's reflective ability made her a special teacher, not just because she had the technical teaching and classroom management skills needed to do things right, but also because she possessed the moral, cultural, and aesthetic understanding needed to help all her students.

ACTION PLAN FOR BECOMING A REFLECTIVE TEACHER

If you are going to become a reflective person and professional, you cannot simply hope for deliverance. You must develop a plan and follow it until technical and critical reflection is a central part of who you are.

Step 1. The first step in preparing a program to become more reflective is to develop the conviction that regular involvement in contemplative activity is worth your time and energy. Helping you build that conviction has been the principal goal of this chapter. We have given you the expert opinion of educational researchers and practitioners regarding the effectiveness of reflection in promoting personal and professional growth. We have shared the stories of teachers regarding their uses of reflection. If you are not convinced of the power of reflection to help you become a better person and teacher, your action plan must stop here. To put it another way, your action plan must begin here; you must find the reasons, collect the evidence, listen to the testimonies, or take whatever action you require to develop the conviction that practicing reflective activities will benefit you, the person and the teacher.

Step 2. Once you have built the conviction that reflection is like breathing—that is, it is necessary for the health of your personal and professional life—you will have little difficulty with Step 2, making time for reflection. We make time for those things in our lives that we highly value. Reflection requires time; in fact, it requires special time every day. It requires time when you can be alone to examine and review, collect and connect your reflections. There are no hard and fast rules about how much time a person must reserve for reflection, but we recommend that beginners plan to set aside some time each day for reflection.

Finding the time for reflection may not be as difficult as finding a quiet place for your reflective activity. This often takes place during the ride home from work, that is, if you turn off your radio and cell phone. Some teachers are able to stay in their room after school for 30 minutes after all the instructional materials have been put away, the classroom chores completed, and the next day's lessons planned. Others like to get away to a serene place at a park, at a library, at home, or in the woods. We know some teachers who have made special arrangements with their spouse and children to respect their request to be left uninterrupted in the office, bedroom, or some other private place at home. One teacher we know spends his private time in the only room with a lock in which he will not be interrupted by doorbells, phone calls, or kids—his bathroom.

Step 3. Once you have found the right place and the special time, you are ready to select the kind of reflective activities that will be most useful for you. In the previous chapter, we suggested that you take a little extra time and record your reflections in your own private journal. You can have a section for recording your private reflections and a section for your school-related reflections.

Hole and McEntee (1999) developed the Guided Reflection Protocol to help teachers improve their teaching. It calls for collecting stories of what has transpired and then responding to the following four questions about one incident:

1. What happened?

2. Why did it happen?

3. What might it mean?

4. What are the implications for my practice?

First, you write down what happened without any attempt at interpretation. Then you seek explanations—there may be more than one. Moving more deeply, you look for significance and finally, move toward future action in light of this analysis.

Some teachers find it valuable to keep their journal or a small note pad beside their bed. They find that those last moments before sleep may often suggest personal and professional brainstorms and creative ideas that are worth recording. When you begin to develop the habit of being reflective, through the process of the daily recording of your ideas, you will be more able to capitalize on those brief or extended moments that present themselves.

For example, Joe is a high school math teacher who has to make a 20-minute commute to and from school each day. He turns off the radio and uses this time, which used to be freeway madness time, for reflection. He has not only found time for reflection, but he has also developed safe driving habits. He stays in the same lane and drives within the posted speed limits.

Jane is another teacher we know, who maintains that if regular reflection is good for her, it must be good for her students as well. She and her students spend the first 10 minutes of their school day in reflective activities. They ponder societal problems; they examine personal dilemmas. They brainstorm solutions; they explore relationships. They write all of their reflections in their daily journal and use these journal reflections as a seedbed for debates, stories, and discussions. If you are convinced that you need to be more reflective but are having problems getting started, look for a colleague, such as Kathy, Jane, or Joe, who would be willing to serve as a reflective teacher mentor for you.

Step 4. Finally, try to evaluate the effectiveness of your reflections in your personal and professional life. Use some of your reflection time to itemize, where possible, the benefits you derive from your commitment to regular personal and professional reflection. An old axiom of school administrators is that "you get what you inspect." If you want your students to be more effective mathematicians, evaluate them regularly to measure their computational and problem-solving skills. If you want to be a more effective person and professional, evaluate the efficacy of your own reflective time.

Jonson (2002) suggests that reflective thinking is most powerful when teachers talk to one another about their ideas. She describes how helpful it is to have an active listener facilitating one's personal growth. Another teacher can provide ongoing emotional and professional support. Portnor (2002) supports the idea of collaborative reflection in that talking with a colleague will encourage you to think more deeply than you would on your own.

Hole and McEntee (1999) developed a structure to use with others in a group process experience—the Critical Incidents Protocol. After participants write down a story, the group reaches a concensus about which story to focus on. The story is read aloud, and the author then answers "clarifying questions" posed by the group: What does this story mean within the larger context of your life? What metaphors stand out for you in the story that represent important themes to you? What are some alternative endings for the story that you considered and rejected? What does this story reveal about your teaching that you value most?

Such questions lead to a deeper discussion of the issues raised in the story, not only for the author, but for everyone in the group. After further conversation in which other participants personalize the themes and discuss the implication for their practice, the group debriefs the process.

Whether conducted individually, with a partner, or in a group, reflection gives you the opportunity to explore in detail the results of your decisions—what went well and why, as well as what needs improvement. Whether daily, weekly, or biweekly, it allows you to analyze past events, acknowledging your accomplishments related to the development of your teaching skills and the successes of your students. You can identify and learn from mistakes in order to change what you do in the future. You may try a different strategy, grouping, or sequence to meet your objectives; observe master teachers address the same concept or skill; read professional journal articles on the topic; or seek additional guidance from others for remediation this year or when the topic comes up next year. It is the reflection on the past that allows you to grow in the future as we look at professional development in the next chapter.

SUGGESTED ACTIVITIES

1. Evaluate how you can be more reflective in your life. Determine when, where, how often, and what format (oral or written) you will follow. Commit to your plan for four months and note how your self-understanding has improved over that period of time.

2. Interview a teacher who is part of a reflective group to learn more about the benefits of focused group interaction.

3. Interview teachers and their mentors to learn more about the benefits of their relationship.

CHAPTER NINE

On Being Passionately Committed

It would be a gross simplification to say that there are only two kinds of educators: those who are committed to the calling of being a teacher and those who are not. It is far more realistic to conceptualize one's degree of commitment to the profession along a continuum. But for purposes of making our point, imagine one group of teachers who have integrated their profession into their lifestyles. They don't do teaching; they are teachers. By contrast, the second group treats teaching as merely a job.

Passionately committed teachers are those who absolutely love what they do. They are constantly searching for more effective ways to reach their children, to master the content and methods of their craft. They feel a personal mission, even a magical quest, to walk through life devouring new experiences, learning as much as they can about the world, about others, about themselves—and helping others to do the same. The second group, the "wake-me-up-when it's-time-to-retire" teachers, view themselves as technicians and see teaching as an easy way to make a living, have summers off, and stand in front of a captive audience who have no choice but to appear to be listening.

We are not interested in fostering the development of ordinary teachers. If you are already a passionately committed veteran, we hope our book validates the daily effort you make to maintain your personal and professional growth. It you are preparing to be a teacher, we hope that you make the ultimate commitment to be as passionate and as superlative a practitioner as you can be, one who inspires young people not just by what you know and can do, but by who you are. If after thoughtfully considering the implications and consequences of choosing to be a teacher, you are still serious about continuing this as a career, we invite you to look at a number of suggestions that most successful practitioners have found helpful in their lives.

We do not offer this advice lightly. In fact, one of the major caveats that we introduce to beginning counselors and teachers is not to give people advice, because only one of two things can result, both of which are pretty awful. First, what if the advice you offer turns out poorly? You will then be blamed by others for ruining their lives, for guiding them to make bad decisions. They will not accept responsibility for the outcome, because you told them what to do. That is why an even more disastrous situation can result if you gave good advice—the person learns to be dependent on you and other authorities for making difficult decisions in the future. You have inadvertently reinforced the ideas, "You don't know what is best for your own life; I do" and "You are not capable enough to find your own way; you need someone else to show you what to do." What the person learns is to go to experts to find out what to do.

Of course, there are times when advice is certainly indicated, such as when someone is about to do something obviously self-destructive and you must respond—but, generally, the first rule of helping is not to give advice; instead, help people find their own answers. This caveat is violated only when you are absolutely certain that what you are offering is exactly what is needed, and there is no other way to help the person to learn the concept involved.

It is therefore with a certain amount of hesitance that we close this book with some very specific advice for you. We present these ideas not as absolute rules we believe you should follow on the path to becoming a passionate, committed teacher; rather they are intended as signposts along the way. They represent a sampling of guidelines that most teachers have found useful in their work and in their lives. We are not saying that if you do these things you will be a wonderful teacher or that you will love your work. As we close the book, this advice to you is meant to represent summary statements of those points we believe are most important in your journey to becoming the ideal teacher you would like to be.

TAKE CARE OF YOURSELF

From the beginning of this book, we have focused on the inseparable linkage between the personal and the professional dimensions of being a teacher. We believe that a satisfied, fully functioning professional must first be a satisfied, well-adjusted person. Your first responsibility, as a person and professional, is to yourself. This is not selfish, narcissistic "me-ism" that we advocate, but a healthy regard for your own well-being, for your own self-esteem. Researchers have demonstrated, again and again, that teachers with high levels of self-esteem are more flexible in their thinking, more willing to learn, and more effective in applying what they learn to improving the learning of their students (Bellon et al., 1992).

BE INTERESTED AND INTERESTING

Remember those few exemplary teachers who inspired you with their many and varied personal and professional qualities? If you looked at them more closely, you would recognize a common trait— they were intensely interested in you and were interesting people. Their passion for lifelong learning fueled their pursuit of new knowledge, new experiences, new opportunities to learn, and their openness to meeting new people. They were risk takers. They brought the world into the classroom for you to explore, examine, and question. They did not have all the answers and were not afraid to let you know that they, like you, were still searching. Their talent was for infecting you with natural curiosity to ask questions and find your own solutions. Because they were interested and interesting people, they had the knack of making education entertaining, and entertainment educational.

Farley (1980) used a traffic light metaphor to characterize people's responses to living and learning. Some people always seem to operate with the yellow light on—living cautious but boring lives.

Others choose the red light and stop their mental motors and spiritual hydraulics. A few passionately committed individuals, however, select the green lights; they take risks and move forward to live interesting lives, regardless of obstacles that may hinder their journey.

FIND A MENTOR

As a beginning teacher, it will be essential for your survival that you find a mentor to guide you through and around the rough spots (Ingersol & Smith, 2003). Find someone who is warm, caring, and has a good sense of humor. You want someone who has time available to spend with you. Select someone who is a good listener and remembers what it is like to be a new teacher.

Teachers new to a school or district as well as veteran teachers can also benefit from the support of special mentors. Do not be afraid to ask for the help of a teacher you admire, someone whom you find to be tremendously interesting, and who you sense has an interest in you.

Guskey (2000) identifies mentoring as one of the major models of professional development that benefits both participants. When paired with a veteran teacher, a less experienced teacher has the opportunity to analyze student learning, identify objectives, examine teaching strategies, and observe each other. According to Guskey, mentoring is most effective when both parties work together to set goals and guidelines for the mentoring relationship.

Teachers who work in isolation from others are more susceptible to burnout and lower levels of self-esteem (Farber & Wechler, 1991; Swick, 1985). Teachers who find mentors and role models to sustain them more often find a synergy, a source of power that enables them to maintain their passionate commitment to teaching (Joyce et al., 2003).

Induction Programs

Most new teachers or teachers new to a district will benefit from an induction program, that is, a formal set of meetings of ongoing support and guidance for at least one school year. Such programs will help you acculturate to the school, district, and community.

These programs vary in length, from weekly to monthly meetings, and they vary in format—open-ended or set topic, such as classroom management or subject area assessment. Often they assign a mentor or support provider to you who will also observe your teaching and work with you to reflect on your practice. They may also help you formulate an individual development plan for the year.

A special feature is that they provide opportunities for you to meet with other new teachers who are having similar experiences. You'll be able to share your successes, learn what works for other teachers, and strategize how to solve common problems as you realize you are not alone in achieving your goal of becoming a teacher.

MAKE LEARNING MEANINGFUL

The best teachers you ever had were not merely those who were smart or who knew a lot; they found myriad ways to make their subjects relevant to your life. Mathematics, science, foreign languages, music, geography, English—no subject will be readily accessible to children unless you can create the means by which they can feel driven to learn it. Unfortunately, you will not learn how to do this in your content courses. You will begin to get ideas in your methods courses. You cannot make something meaningful for anyone; that is a task for each student.

You can, however, spend as much time and energy helping students to understand why they are studying a particular subject and how it will benefit them as you do any other aspect of the learning process. The best teachers are those who have infused their students with the passionate desire to learn what they have to offer. Period.

INSTILL YOUR TEACHING WITH CREATIVE ARTISTRY

As a teacher, you are likely to be more effective in making learning relevant if you infuse your instruction and classroom environment with genuine creativity. You do not have to be a Picasso to enliven your classroom with art. You do not have to be a Mozart to use music to promote lively student responses. As a teacher, you must decide what media to select to reach your intended outcomes with students. Creative teachers select from a variety of choices, including audio (music, tape recordings), video (overheads, slides, still pictures), kinesthetic (math manipulatives, science lab materials), and mixed media (videotapes, movies, Web-based instruction).

BALANCE CARING AND CONTROLLING

You can probably remember some caring teachers whose classrooms were pits of disorder. On the other extreme, you may also have experienced controlling tyrants who displayed little caring for students. As a passionately committed teacher, you will work to balance these two important dimensions of teaching. Caring and controlling are not conflicting opposites; they are mutually supportive (McLaughlin, 1991). "The core of effective teacher and student relationships is a healthy balance between dominance and cooperation" (Marzano, 2003, p. 49). It is the teacher's responsibility to work with students to establish the classroom boundaries that will promote self-discipline and encourage teachers and students to mutually respect and care for each other. Always remember: Your mission as an educator is not just to produce children who know things, but to grow children who can think for themselves, who can solve problems ingeniously, who can take our current base of knowledge and move beyond it.

CULTIVATE YOUR CULTURAL SENSITIVITY

In North America, as in most of the world, nations are becoming more and more culturally diverse. We are composed of many subcultures with citizens who have the freedom to express their ideas, beliefs, and lifestyles. Ignorance and fear frequently prevent us from appreciating the variety of cultural traits and beliefs of other people. It is a part of the passionately committed teacher's moral responsibility to cultivate knowledge and appreciation of cultural diversity and to teach others to do the same.

Unfortunately, so many efforts related to cultural sensitivity and culturally responsive teaching practices are embedded in political correctness and token gestures that have little lasting impact (Kottler, 1997b). It takes real passion to transcend the minimal efforts that are often part of school district policies and to deal with real issues of racism, prejudice, and social justice. Once again, this involves far more than mere talk and attending a few inservice workshops; it means practicing in your life the sort of commitment to diversity that you hope for your students to have.

BECOME INVOLVED IN SCHOOL AND DISTRICT ACTIVITIES

There are many ways to flame the passion of your commitment. As mentioned earlier, we strongly encourage you to participate in school activities after school as coach or sponsor or part of the audience as your time permits. At the school level, there will be opportunities for committee involvement, such as accreditation, school improvement, professional development, not to mention parent-teacher-student associations. At the district level, there may be committees for textbook selection, curriculum development, assessment, induction programs, and advisory boards.

CONTINUE YOUR EDUCATION

There are many reasons for continuing your education. Expanding your professional base will enhance your effectiveness as you upgrade your skills and become aware of new developments in your field. Additional education will meet your needs for intellectual stimulation and forming new relationships. At the same time additional degrees will likely result in increases on district salary scales. To maintain teaching licenses, states require a minimum of university credits or professional development credits. Many school districts today offer induction programs for which participants as new teachers and mentors may receive university credit toward a M.A. or M.S. degree.

BECOME ACTIVE IN PROFESSIONAL ORGANIZATIONS

There are many outstanding professional organizations you can join that will help sustain the idealism of your passionate commitment. There are national councils of teachers of English, mathematics, science, and social studies, with local, state, and national organizations. A list of general and specialized professional organizations is provided at the end of this chapter (p. 158). There are other specialty organizations for teachers of early childhood education, reading, special education, bilingual education, and physical education. There are major professional organizations that aim is provide support for educators in the areas of curriculum, instruction, supervision, and staff development. You may also find that it is not difficult for enthusiastic educators to be nominated for one or more honorary educational organizations with Greek designations such as Kappa Delta Pi and Kappa Delta Epsilon (KDE) or belonging to an international association of professional educators such as Phi Delta Kappa (PDK).

You can attend the annual conferences of these professional organizations; mingle with other passionately committed teachers; and keep on the cutting edge of pedagogical knowledge, practice, and research. You can broaden your passionate commitment by serving in a leadership role as an officer in a professional organization. You can also find many resources for improving your teaching, conducting research, and enriching your personal and professional life through your membership in professional organizations. Many of these professional organizations publish outstanding journals and educational materials useful to classroom teachers.

TOWARD CLOSURE

There is no closure, no finish line, no book's end in the quest to become and continue to be a caring, competent, and passionately committed teacher. It is the work of a lifetime. For you, this may be the very beginning of a journey that is at once exhilarating, frightening, exciting, and overwhelming or you may be already on your way. Where will you be a year from now? Five years? Fifteen years? Thirty years? To be a teacher, a really fine teacher, the kind of teacher that you always wanted to be—one who is loved and respected—is the most difficult task you will ever undertake. As much as you study and learn, as hard as you try, as much time and energy as you devote to this priority, you will still never get close to the potential you have to inspire others. That is the enigma of education: The best job you can do is not nearly enough for what children deserve.

Teaching is one of the most rewarding professions. We hope that we have motivated you to become a committed, passionate educator willing to pursue the relationship skills needed for being an effective teacher and an effective human being. Whatever your reason for entering or continuing in the profession, your love for children, a sense of fulfillment in sharing the discovery of knowledge, enjoyment of learning, desire to give back to community, you will find your relationships enhanced when you concentrate on the human dimension of teaching.

SUGGESTED ACTIVITIES

1. Observe passionate teachers. Discuss how they maintain their energy and ambition.

2. Evaluate how well you are taking care of yourself. Is there balance in your life between work and family? Do you get enough sleep? Do you take time to exercise? Are you pursuing a hobby or other interests? Are you planning for your future? Do you take time for reflection?

3. Interview people from various cultures to speak about their customs and experiences. Or, immerse yourself in another culture.

4. Join a general or specialized educational professional organization related to your content area. Find out when and where their meetings and annual conference take place. Their publications will keep you abreast of current practices in the field. Their Web sites will offer additional resources.

Professional Organizations

General Professional Organizations

American Federation of Teachers	www.aft.org
Association for Supervision and Curriculum Development	www.ascd.org
National Board for Professional Teaching Standards	www.nbpts.org/standards
National Education Association	www.nea.org
Phi Delta Kappa	www.pdkintl.org

(Continued)

Professional Organizations: (Continued)

Specialized Professional Organizations

American Council for the Teaching of Foreign Languages	www.actfl.org/i4a/pages/index.cfm?pageid=1
American Alliance for Health, Physical Education, Recreation and Dance	www.aahperd.org
American Alliance for Theater and Education	www.aate.com
American Association of Teachers of French	http://www.frenchteachers.org/
American Association of Teachers of German	www.aatg.org
American Association of Teachers of Spanish and Portuguese	www.aatsp.org
American Choral Directors Association	www.acda.org
Association for the Advancement of Arts Education	http://www.artslynx.org/artsed/
Council for Exceptional Children	www.cec.sped.org/
International Reading Association	www.reading.org
Music Educators National Conference	www.menc.org
National Art Education Association	www.naea-reston.org
National Business Education Association	www.nbea.org
National Council for the Social Studies	www.ncss.org
National Council of Teachers of English	www.ncte.org
National Council of Teachers of Mathematics	www.nctm.org
National Science Teachers Association	www.nsta.org

References and Suggested Readings

Abell, S. K., Dillon, D. R., Hopkins, C. J., McInerney, W. D., & O'Brien, D. G. (1995). Somebody to count on: Mentor/intern relationships in a beginning teacher internship program. *Teaching and Teacher Education, 11,* 173–188.

Abrams, L. M., & Madaus, G. F. (2003). The lessons of high-stakes testing. *Educational Leadership, 61*(3), 31–35.

Alder, N., & Moulton, M. (1998). Caring relationships: Perspectives from middle school students. *Research in Middle Level Education Quarterly, 21*(3), 15–32.

Anderson, R. (1984). Some reflections on the acquisition of knowledge. *Educational Researcher, 13*(9), 5–10.

Armstrong, D. G., Hensen, K. T., & Savage, T. V. (2005). *Teaching today: An introduction to education* (7th ed.). Upper Saddle River, NJ: Pearson Education.

Banks, J. (1993). *Multiethnic education* (3rd ed.). Boston: Allyn & Bacon.

Barrell, B. (1991). Classroom artistry. *Educational Forum, 55*(4), 333–342.

Beck, J. S., & Beck, A. (1995). *Cognitive therapy: Basics and beyond.* New York: Guilford.

Bellon, J., Bellon, E., & Blank, M. (1992). *Teaching from a research knowledge base.* New York: Merrill.

Bemak, F., & Keys, S. (2000). *Violent and aggressive youth.* Thousand Oaks, CA: Corwin.

Ben-Yosef, E. (2003). Respecting students' cultural literacies. *Educational Leadership, 61*(2), 80–82.

Bigge, M. L., & Shermis, S. S. (1998). *Learning theories for teachers* (6th ed.). Reading, MA: Addison-Wesley.

Birch, S. H., & Ladd, G. W. (1997). Teacher-child relationship and children's early school adjustment. *Journal of School Psychology, 35,* 61–79.

Blacker, D. J. (1997). *Dying to teach: The educator's search for immortality.* New York: Columbia University Press.

Blase, J. (1991). *The politics of life in schools: Power, conflict, and cooperation.* Newbury Park, CA: Sage.

Blase, J., & Kirby, P. (1999). *Bringing out the best in teachers: What effective principals do* (2nd ed.). Thousand Oaks, CA: Corwin.

Borich, G. (2004). *Effective teaching methods* (4th ed.). Upper Saddle River, NJ: Merrill.

Boy, A., & Pine, G. (1971). *Expanding the self: Personal growth for teachers.* Dubuque, IA: William C. Brown.

Bradshaw, J. (1990). *Home coming: Reclaiming and championing your inner child.* New York: Bantam.

Brandt, R. (1986). On the expert teacher: A conversation with David Berliner. *Educational Leadership, 44*(2), 4–9.

Brock, S. E. (1998). Helping classrooms cope with traumatic events. *Professional School Counseling, 2,* 110–116.

Brooks, J. G., & Brooks, M. G. (1999). *In search of understanding: The case for constructivist classrooms* (2nd ed.). Alexandria, VA: Association for Supervision and Curriculum Development.

Brown, J., Collins, A., & Duguid, O. (1989). Situated cognition and the culture of learning. *Educational Researcher, 18*(1), 32–72.

Bryk, A., & Schneider, B. (2003). Trust in schools: A core resource for school reform. *Educational Leadership, 60*(6), 40–44.

Burns, D. (1999). *Feeling good: The new mood therapy* (2nd ed.). New York: HarperCollins.

Buzzell, J. B. (1996). *School and family partnerships.* Albany, NY: Delmar.

Campbell, A. (1998). Keep an eye on the class clown. *Learning, 26,* 20–23.

Campbell, D. E., & Delgado-Campbell, D. (2000). *Choosing democracy: A practical guide to multicultural education* (2nd ed.). Upper Saddle River, NJ: Merrill.

Carkhuff, R., & Berenson, D. (1981). *The skilled teacher.* Amherst, MA: Human Development Resource Press.

Cleaver, E. (1968). *Soul on ice.* New York: Dell.

Cohen, E. G., & Goodlad, J. I. (1994). *Designing groupwork: Strategies for the heterogeneous classroom* (2nd ed.). New York: Teachers College Press.

Cohen, F. (1972). Interracial interaction disability. *Human Relations, 25,* 9–24.

Coles, R. (1990). *The spiritual life of children.* Boston: Houghton Mifflin.

Conroy, P. (1982). *The lords of discipline.* New York: Bantam.

Covey, S. (1999). *Living the seven habits: Stories of courage and inspiration.* New York: Fireside.

Damon, W. (2000). *Social, emotional, and personality development.* New York: Wiley.

Dantonio, M. (1998). Perfecting the art of teaching. *Learning, 26,* 35–37.

Darling-Hammond, L. (2003). Keeping good teachers: Why it matters, what leaders can do. *Educational Leadership, 60*(8), 6–13.

Dewey, J. (1965). Theory and practice in education. In M. Borromann (Ed.), *Teacher education in America: A documentary history,* New York: Teachers College Press.

Dworkin, A. (1987). *Teacher burnout in the public schools: Structural causes and consequences for children.* Albany: State University of New York Press.

Eby, J. W., Herrell, A. L., & Hicks, J. (2001). *Reflective planning, teaching, and evaluation: K-12* (2nd ed.). Englewood Cliffs, NJ: Prentice Hall.

Egan, G. (2004). *The skilled helper: A problem-management and opportunity–development approach to helping* (7th ed.). Pacific Grove, CA: Brooks/Cole.

Ellis, A. (1997). *The practice of rational emotive behavior therapy.* New York: Springer.

Ellis, A. (1998). *A guide to rational living* (3rd ed.). New York: Wilshire Books.

Farber, B. A., & Wechler, L. D. (1991). *Crisis in education: Stress and burnout in the American teacher.* San Francisco: Jossey-Bass.

Erwin, J. (2003). Giving students what they need. *Educational Leadership, 61*(1), 19–23.

Farley, C. (1980). *When the light turns green . . . Go.* Costa Mesa, CA: Excellence.

Forey, W. F., Christensen, O. J., & England, J. T. (1994). Teacher burnout: A relationship with Holland and Adlerian typologies. *Individual Psychology, 50,* 3–16.

Freudenberger, H. J. (1974). Staff burnout. *Journal of Social Issues, 30,* 159–165.

Friesen, D., Prokop, C., & Sarros, J. (1988). Why teachers burn out. *Educational Research Quarterly, 12*(3), 9–19.

Gardner, H. (1993). *Frames of mind: The theory of multiple intelligences.* New York: Basic Books.

Gardner, H. (1999). *Intelligence refrained: Multiple intelligences for the 21st century.* New York: Basic Books.

Gazda, G. M., Asbury, F. R. , Balzer, F. J., Childers, W. C., & Phelps, R. E. (1998). *Human relations development: A manual for educators.* Boston: Allyn & Bacon.

Getzels, J., & Jackson, D. (1962). *Creativity and intelligence: Explorations with gifted students.* New York: Wiley.

Ghaye, A., & Ghaye, K. (1998). *Teaching and learning through critical reflective practice.* Philadelphia: Taylor & Francis.

Gill, V. (1998). *The ten commandments of good teaching.* Thousand Oaks, CA: Corwin.

Glantz, K., & Pearce, J. (1989). *Exiles from Eden: Psychotherapy front an evolutionary perspective.* New York: Norton.

Glasser, W. (1998). *The quality school* (3rd ed.). New York: HarperCollins.

Glasser, W., & Dotson, K. L. (1998). *Choice theory in the classroom.* New York: Harper.

Gmelch, W. (1983). Stress for success: How to optimize your performance. *Theory into practice, 22*(1), 7–14.

Goethals, M. S., Howard, R. A., & Sanders, M. M. (2003). *Student teaching: A process approach to reflective practice* (2nd ed.). Englewood Cliffs, NJ: Prentice Hall.

Gold, Y. (1988). Recognizing and coping with academic burnout. *Contemporary Education, 59*(3), 142–145.

Goldberg, M. F. (2004). The test mess. *Phi Delta Kappan, 85*(5) 361–366.

Goodlad, J. I. (1990). *Teachers for our nation's schools.* San Francisco: Jossey-Bass.

Goodlad, J. I. (1998). *Educational renewal: Better teachers, better schools.* San Francisco: Jossey-Bass.

Gordon, T. (1974). *Teacher effectiveness training.* New York: David McKay.

Guillaume, A. (2004). *K-12 classroom teaching: A primer for new professionals* (2nd ed.). Upper Saddle River, NJ: Pearson Prentice Hall.

Guskey, T. R. (2000). *Evaluating professional development.* Thousand Oaks, CA: Corwin.

Hart, L. (1983). *Human brain and human learning,* Oak Creek, AZ: Books for Educators.

Hazler, R. J. (1998). *Helping in the hallways: Advanced strategies for enhancing school relationships.* Thousand Oaks, CA: Corwin.

Hearron, P., & Hildebrand, V. (2004). *Guiding young children* (7th ed.). Englewood Cliffs, NJ: Prentice Hall.

Henderson, J. G. (Ed.). (1996). *Reflective teaching: The study of your constructivist practices* (2nd ed.). Englewood Cliffs, NJ: Prentice Hall.

Hendrick, L. (1997). *Total learning* (5th ed.). Englewood Cliffs, NJ: Prentice Hall.

Hernandez, H. (2000). *Multicultural education: A teacher's guide to context, process, and content* (2nd ed.). Englewood Cliffs, NJ: Prentice Hall.

Hewson, P., & Hewson, M. (1988). An appropriate conception of teaching science: A view from studies of science learning. *Science Education, 72*(5), 597–614.

Hole, S., & McEntee, G. H. (1999). Reflection is at the heart of practice. *Educational Leadership, 56*(8), 34–37.

Holt, J. (1964). *How children fail.* New York: Pitman.

Holt, J. (1968). *How children learn.* New York: Dell.

Horowitz, F., & O'Brien, M. (Eds.). (1985). *The gifted and talented: Developmental perspectives.* Washington, DC: American Psychological Association.

Humphrey, J., & Humphrey, J. (1986). *Coping with stress in teaching.* New York: AMS Press.

Ingersoll, R. M. (1996). Teachers' decision-making power and school conflict. *Sociology of Education, 69,* 159–176.

Ingersoll, R. M., & Smith, T. M. (2003). The wrong solution to the teacher shortage. *Educational Leadership, 60*(8), 30–33.

Jackson, J. T., & Bynum, N. (1998). Drama: A teaching tool for culturally diverse children with behavioral disorders. *Journal of Instructional Psychology, 24,* 158–166.

Jesild, A. (1955). *When teachers face themselves.* New York: Teachers College Press.

Johnson, D. W., & Johnson, R. T. (1996). Conflict resolution and peer mediation programs in elementary and secondary schools: A review of the research, *Review of Educational Research, 66,* 459–506.

Johnson, D. W., & Johnson, R. T. (1999). *Learning together and alone* (5th ed.). Boston: Allyn & Bacon.

Jones, F. (1987). *Positive classroom discipline.* New York: McGraw-Hill.

Jonson, K. (2002). *Being an effective mentor.* Thousand Oaks, CA: Corwin.

Joyce, B., & Showers, B. (1983). *Power in staff development through research on training.* Alexandria, VA: Association for Supervision and Curriculum Development.

Joyce, B., Weil, M., Calhoun, E., & Joyce, B. (2003). *Models of teaching* (7th ed.). New York: Simon & Schuster.

Kaikai, S., & Kaikai, R. (1990, February 28–March 3). *Positive ways to avoid instructor burnout.* Paper presented at the National Conference on Successful College Teaching, Orlando, FL.

Karns, M. (1994). *How to create positive relationships with students.* New York: Research Press.

Kauchak, D., & Eggen, P. (2005). *Introduction to teaching: Becoming a professional* (2nd ed.). Upper Saddle River, NJ: Pearson Education.

Kleiner, C. (1998, October 26). Make room for sergeants. *U.S. News and World Report,* 69–70.

Kosier, K. (1998). *Discipline checklist: Preparing for today's difficult students.* Washington, DC: National Education Association.

Kottler, E., & Kottler, J. A. (2002). *Children with limited English: Teaching strategies for the regular classroom* (2nd ed.). Thousand Oaks, CA: Corwin.

Kottler, E., Kottler, J. A., & Kottler, C. (2004). *Secrets for secondary school teachers: How to succeed in your first year* (2nd ed.). Thousand Oaks, CA: Corwin.

Kottler, J., & Brown, R. (2003). *Introduction to therapeutic counseling: Voices from the field* (5th ed.). Pacific Grove, CA: Brooks/Cole.

Kottler, J. A. (1990). *Private moments, secret selves: Enriching our time alone.* New York: Ballantine.

Kottler, J. A. (1993). *On being a therapist* (2nd ed.). San Francisco: Jossey-Bass.

Kottler, J. A. (1994). *Beyond blame: A new way of resolving conflict in relationships.* San Francisco: Jossey-Bass.

Kottler, J. A. (1997a). *Travel that can change your life.* San Francisco: Jossey-Bass.

Kottler, J. A. (1997b). *What's really said in the teachers lounge: Provocative ideas about cultures and classrooms.* Thousand Oaks, CA: Corwin

Kottler, J. A. (2000). *Doing good: Passion and commitment for helping others.* Philadelphia: Accelerated Development.

Kottler, J. A. (2001). *Learning group leadership: An experiential approach.* Boston: Allyn & Bacon.

Kottler, J. A. (2002). *Students who drive you crazy: Succeeding with resistant, unmotivated, and otherwise difficult young people.* Thousand Oaks, CA: Corwin.

Kottler, J. A., & Kottler, E. (2000). *Counseling skills for teachers.* Thousand Oaks, CA: Corwin.

Kriete, R. (2003). Start the day with community. *Educational Leadership, 61*(1) 68–70.

Leathers, D. (1996). *Successful nonverbal communication: Principles and applications.* (3rd ed.). Boston: Allyn & Bacon.

Manning, M. L., & Baruth, L. G. (1999). *Multicultural education of children and adolescents* (3rd ed.). Boston: Allyn & Bacon.

Marlowe, B. A., & Page, M. L. (1998). *Creating and sustaining the constructive classroom.* Thousand Oaks, CA: Corwin.

Marshall, S. (1991). The voice of experience. *Educational Forum, 55*(2), 107–121.

Marzano, R. J. (2003). *What works in schools: Translating research into action.* Alexandria, VA: ASCD.

Maslach, C. (1982). *Burnout: The cost of caring.* Englewood Cliffs, NJ: Prentice Hall.

Maslach, C., & Jackson, S. (1981). The measurement of experienced burnout. *Journal of Occupational Behavior, 2,* 99–113.

Maslach, C., & Leiter, M. P. (1997). *The truth about burnout.* San Francisco: Jossey-Bass.

Maslow, A. (1968). *Toward a psychology of being.* Princeton, NJ: Van Nostrand.

Maxim, G. (1997). *The very young* (5th ed.). Englewood Cliffs, NJ: Prentice Hall.

McCroskey, J., & Richmond, V. (1992). *Power in the classroom: Communication, control and concern.* Hillsdale, NJ: Erlbaum.

McLaughlin, H. (1991). Reconciling care and control: Authority in classroom relationships. *Journal of Teacher Education, 42*(3), 182–195.

McQualter, J. (1985). Becoming a teacher: Preservice teacher education using personal construct theory. *Journal of Education for Teaching, 11*(2), 177–186.

Meek, A. (1991). On thinking about teaching: A conversation with Eleanor Duckworth. *Educational Leadership, 49*(6), 30–34.

Mendes, E. (2003). What empathy can do. *Educational Leadership, 61*(1) 56–59.

Miller, P. C., & Endo, H. (2004). Understanding and meeting the needs of ESL students. *Phi Delta Kappan, 85*(10), 786–791.

Mills, R. A., Powell, R. R., & Pollack, J. P. (1992). The influence of middle level interdisciplinary teaming on teacher isolation: A case study. *Research in Middle Level Education, 15*(2), 9–25.

Mintzes, J. J., Wandersee, J. A., & Novak, J. D. (Eds.). (1998). *Teaching science for understanding: A human constructivist view.* New York: Academic Press.

Montgomery, M. J. (1999). *Building bridges with parents.* Thousand Oaks, CA: Corwin.

Moustakas, C. (1986). Being in, being for, and being with. *Humanistic Psychologist, 14*(2), 100–104.

Nelson-Jones, R. (1990). *Human-relationships: A skills approach.* Pacific Grove, CA: Brooks/Cole.

Noddings, N. (1984). *Caring: A feminist approach to ethics and moral education.* Berkeley: University of California Press.

Noel, J. (1999). *Sources: Notable selections in multicultural education.* New York: McGraw-Hill.

Norton, J. L. (1993). Creative thinking and the reflective practitioner. *Journal of Instructional Psychology, 21*, 139–147.

Olewus, D. (2003). A profile of bullying at school. *Educational Leadership, 60*(6), 12–17.

Orlich, D. C., Harder, R. J., Callahan, R. C., Kauchak, D. P., Pendergrass, R. A., Keogh, A. J., & Gibson, H. (1990). *Teaching strategies: A guide to better instruction,* (3rd ed.). Lexington, MA: D. C. Heath.

Palmer, P. (1998). *The courage to teach.* San Francisco: Jossey-Bass.

Parkay, F. W., & Stanford, B. H. (2001). *Becoming a Teacher.* Boston: Allyn and Bacon.

Pedulla, J. J. (2003). State-mandated testing: What do teachers think? *Educational Leadership, 61*(3), 42–46.

Phillips-Hershey, E., & Kanagy, B. (1996). Teaching students to manage personal anger constructively. *Elementary School Guidance and Counseling, 30*, 228–234.

Portner, H. (2002). *Mentoring new teachers.* Thousand Oaks, CA: Corwin.

Powell, R., McLaughlin, H., Savage, T., & Zehm, S. (1999). *Management for culturally diverse classrooms: Understanding the social curriculum.* Englewood Cliffs, NJ: Prentice Hall.

Powell, R., Zehm, S., & Kottler, J. (1995). *Classrooms under the influence: Counteracting problems of addiction.* Thousand Oaks, CA: Corwin.

Progoff, I. (1975). *At a journal workshop.* New York: Dialogue House.

Rist, R. (1974). Student, social class and teacher expectations: The self-fulfilling prophecy in ghetto education. *Harvard Educational Review, 40,* 1–451.

Rogers, C. (1939). *The clinical treatment of the problem child.* Boston: Houghton Mifflin.

Rogers, C. (1969a). *Freedom to learn.* Columbus, OH: Charles C. Merrill.

Rogers, C. (1969b). What it means to become a person. In F. Natalicio & C. Hereford (Eds.), *The teacher as a person.* Dubuque, IA: William C. Brown.

Rogers, C. (1980). *A way of being.* Boston: Houghton Mifflin

Rosenholtz, S. (1985). Treating problems of academic status. In J. Berger & M. Zeiditch Jr. (Eds.), *Status, rewards, and influence.* San Francisco: Jossey-Bass.

Rubin, L. (1989). The thinking teacher: Cultivating pedagogical intelligence. *Journal of Teacher Education, 40*(6), 31–34.

Ryan, K., & Cooper, J. (2004). *Those who can, teach* (10th ed.). Boston: Houghton Mifflin.

Saunders, W. (1992). The constructivist perspective: Implications and teaching strategies for science. *School Science and Mathematics, 92*(3), 137–140.

Schaps, E. (2003). Creating a school community. *Educational Leadership, 60*(6), 31–33.

Scheidecker, D., & Freeman, W. (1999). *Bringing out the best in students.* Thousand Oaks, CA: Corwin.

Schon, D. (1990). *The reflective practitioner: How professionals think in action.* New York: Basic Books.

Schon, D. (1987). *Educating the reflective practitioner.* San Francisco: Jossey-Bass.

Schunk, D. H. (1999). *Learning theories: An educational perspective.* Englewood Cliffs, NJ: Prentice Hall.

Selley, N. (1999). *The art of constructivist teaching in the primary school.* London: David Fulton Publisher.

Sergiovanni, T. (1992). *Moral leadership: Getting to the heart of school reform.* San Francisco: Jossey-Bass.

Skinner, B. F. (1969). Why teachers fail. In F. Natalicio & C. Hereford (Eds.), *The teacher as a person.* Dubuque, IA: William C. Brown.

Sklare, G. B. (1997). *Brief counseling that works.* Thousand Oaks, CA: Corwin.

Slavin, R. (1988). *Student team learning: An overview and practical guide.* Washington, DC: National Education Association.

Slavin, R. E. (2002). *Educational psychology: Theory and practice* (7th ed.). Boston: Allyn & Bacon.

Smyth, L. (1989). Developing and sustaining initial reflection in teacher education. *Journal of Teacher Education, 40*(2), 2–9.

Sparks-Langer, G., & Colton, A. (1991). Synthesis of research on teachers' reflective thinking. *Educational Leadership, 48*(6), 37–44.

Spaulding, C. (1992). *Motivation in the classroom.* New York: McGraw-Hill.

Stone, R. (1999). *Best classroom practices.* Thousand Oaks, CA: Corwin

Studer, J. (1996). Understanding and preventing aggressive responses in youth. *Elementary School Guidance and Counseling, 30*, 194–203.

Swick, K. *(1985). Stress and the classroom teacher.* Washington, DC: National Education Association.

Taffel, R. (1999, September-October). Discovering our children. *Family Therapy Networker,* 24–35.

Teacher shortage. (n.d.). Retrieved June 27, 2004, from the National Education Web site at www.nea.org/teachershortage/03shortagefact-sheet.html

Tom, A. (1985). Inquiring into inquiry-oriented teacher education. *Journal of Teacher Education, 36*(5), 35–44.

Villa, R., & Townsend, J. (1993). Making inclusive education work. *Educational Leadership, 61*(2), 19–23.

Weissbourd, R. (2003). Moral teachers, moral students. *Educational Leadership, 60*(6), 6–11.

Wilde, S. (1997). To be a good person. *Learning, 26*, 38–42.

Willard-Holt, C. (2003). Raising expectations for the gifted. *Educational Leadership, 61*(2), 72–75.

Williams, J. S. (2003). Why great teachers stay. *Educational Leadership, 60*(8), 71–74.

Wolk, S. (2003). Hearts and minds. *Educational Leadership, 61*(1), 14–18.

Wyatt, R. L., & Looper, S. (2003). *So you have to have a portfolio: A teacher's guide to preparation and presentation* (2nd ed.). Thousand Oaks, CA: Corwin.

Yell, M. L., & Drasgow, E. (2005). *No child left behind: A guide for professionals.* Upper Saddle River, NJ: Pearson Education.

Zeichner, K., & Liston, D. *(1987).* Teaching student teachers to reflect. *Harvard Educational Review, 57*(1), 23–48.

Zeichner, K. M., & Liston, D. P. (1996). *Reflective teaching: An introduction.* Mahwah, NJ: Erlbaum.

Index

**CORWIN
PRESS**

The Corwin Press logo—a raven striding across an open book—represents the union of courage and learning. Corwin Press is committed to improving education for all learners by publishing books and other professional development resources for those serving the field of K–12 education. By providing practical, hands-on materials, Corwin Press continues to carry out the promise of its motto: **"Helping Educators Do Their Work Better."**